CW00348004

About Island Press

Since 1984, the nonprofit Island Press has been stimulating, shaping, and communicating the ideas that are essential for solving environmental problems worldwide. With more than 800 titles in print and some 40 new releases each year, we are the nation's leading publisher on environmental issues. We identify innovative thinkers and emerging trends in the environmental field. We work with world-renowned experts and authors to develop cross-disciplinary solutions to environmental challenges.

Island Press designs and implements coordinated book publication campaigns in order to communicate our critical messages in print, in person, and online using the latest technologies, programs, and the media. Our goal: to reach targeted audiences—scientists, policymakers, environmental advocates, the media, and concerned citizens—who can and will take action to protect the plants and animals that enrich our world, the ecosystems we need to survive, the water we drink, and the air we breathe.

Island Press gratefully acknowledges the support of its work by the Agua Fund, Inc., The Margaret A. Cargill Foundation, Betsy and Jesse Fink Foundation, The William and Flora Hewlett Foundation, The Kresge Foundation, The Forrest and Frances Lattner Foundation, The Andrew W. Mellon Foundation, The Curtis and Edith Munson Foundation, The Overbrook Foundation, The David and Lucile Packard Foundation, The Summit Foundation, Trust for Architectural Easements, The Winslow Foundation, and other generous donors.

The opinions expressed in this book are those of the author(s) and do not necessarily reflect the views of our donors.

Completing Our Streets

COMPLETING OUR STREETS

The Transition to Safe and Inclusive
Transportation Networks

Barbara McCann

 ISLANDPRESS

Washington | Covelo | London

Library of Congress Cataloging-in-Publication Data
McCann, Barbara.
Completing our streets : the transition to safe and inclusive transportation networks / by Barbara McCann.
     pages cm
Includes bibliographical references and index.
ISBN-13: 978-1-61091-430-7 (cloth : alk. paper)
ISBN-10: 1-61091-430-9 (cloth : alk. paper)
ISBN-13: 978-1-61091-431-4 (pbk. : alk. paper)
ISBN-10: 1-61091-431-7 (pbk. : alk. paper) 1. Urban transportation policy--United States--Citizen participation. 2. Streets--United States--Planning. 3. Traffic safety--United States--Planning. 4. City planning--United States--Citizen participation. I. Title.
HE308.M38 2013
388.4'110973--dc23

Printed on recycled, acid-free paper

Manufactured in the United States of America
10 9 8 7 6 5 4 3 2 1

Keywords: AASHTO green book, accessibility, active living, automobile Level of Service, green streets, ISTEA, MAP-21, Metropolitan Planning Organization (MPO), National Complete Streets Coalition, pedestrian safety, performance measures, Safe Routes to School (SRTS), transportation demand management (TDM), transportation equity, transportation finance, transportation maintenance and operations, transportation planning, transportation reform, transportation safety, walkability

To the memory of Susie Stephens, who planted a seed

Contents

Buford Highway, Atlanta, Georgia. Note the trail leading to the bus stop in the background. (Photo by Steve Davis.)

Preface

ONE DAY IN THE EARLY 1990S, I was riding my bicycle in Atlanta along wide, fast-moving Ponce de Leon Avenue. I was passing by Ponce de Leon Plaza, Atlanta's very first strip shopping center, sharing one of the six lanes with cars speeding by, inches away. I began to imagine a city with bike lanes everywhere. It turned out to be more than a fleeting thought.

I had been helping organize an annual Bike to Work Day effort that brought out a few stalwarts, but most people reacted to the suggestion that they bike to work with skepticism or disbelief. If you could afford it, driving was the default for almost all trips in Atlanta, even to reach transit. MARTA (Metropolitan Atlanta Rapid Transit Authority) rail stations were surrounded with parking lots and ringed with fences to keep people from walking straight into adjoining neighborhoods—if you were using transit, you must be up to no good. Bicycling was assumed to require a separate path, because the roads were clearly no place for anyone outside of a car. I knew that encouragement alone was not going to get Atlantans to try bicycling. They needed the road network to give them some space.

This was at the time when Atlanta was just starting to understand the downside of its explosive outward growth. Just a few years earlier, the Georgia Department of Transportation had confidently launched a massive highway expansion project to "Free the Freeways"—and the interstates were again jammed. The region was threatened with losing control of its federal transportation dollars due to its failure to come up with a plan to reduce automobile emissions. I became fascinated by the struggle to change the course of development and transportation investments. Shortly thereafter, the Atlanta region did become the first and only metro area in the nation to lose control of its federal gas tax money because of Clean Air Act violations. The term *sprawl* was just coming into vogue, and I realized these issues were not isolated to Atlanta. I was working as a writer and producer at CNN, so I did what any journalist would do—I started researching and reporting.

Not long after completing an hour-long special for CNN on transportation and development issues, I took a job at a Washington, DC, nonprofit, the Surface Transportation Policy Project (STPP), which worked to defend and expand innovations in federal transportation funding to allow more spending on motorized modes and public transportation. I wrote widely publicized research reports about how transportation planning decisions affect Americans' quality of life, from endangering pedestrians to forcing moms to become chauffeurs. And as I talked to reporters, planners, and local leaders, I realized how hard it was for people to envision places where driving was not an everyday necessity, or roadways where bicycles, public transportation, pedestrians, and cars could coexist.

New urbanism and smart growth were starting to present an alternative. The idea of traffic calming to slow cars was gaining ground, and a few places were building bike lanes and light rail. But each project was still a struggle, against attitudes, assumptions, and systems designed to deliver auto-mobility.

People from the public health community visited STPP in 2000, having come to the conclusion I had reached in Atlanta: asking people to get out and walk or bicycle was hopeless until we could start building places that were safe and inviting to walk and bike. They suspected the growing obesity epidemic had something to do with Americans' ability to move around without actually moving their bodies. With funding from the Robert Wood Johnson Foundation, I worked with transportation researcher Reid Ewing on a study finding that people who live in more sprawling places are more likely to be overweight or obese.[1] The study was the first to use national health and land use data to make a connection between sprawl and health. The companion report received extensive media coverage in 2003, setting up a conversation that has continued since.[2]

What This Book Does Not Do

The previous summary is the background that led to my creation of the Complete Streets movement, and I tell it in part to explain what this book doesn't do. It doesn't dwell on the problems of our automobile-oriented system. I explored those issues earlier in my career, and many others have written articulate, well-researched books and articles on the topic. I encourage you to explore them, and I provide some resources in the bibliography. This book will make only a limited case for why and how compact communities with transportation choices create healthier, more vibrant, and more sustainable communities. The National Complete Streets Coalition has developed (and keeps updated) an extensive list of fact sheets and reports that are chock-full of statistics and information (see appendix B for a guide to these resources). Island Press and many others have also developed extensive resources that do this job.

This book also does not paint a vision of an ideal future or provide a template for the "perfect complete street." This book is not the cutting-edge design manifesto that some people may expect. Plenty of others have created beautiful, innovative templates for multimodal streets and compact, walkable towns and neighborhoods. But I've found that those finely crafted visions are not of much immediate use in the communities I see as my baseline: Atlanta and the small towns across Georgia and the suburban United States. These places, and so many more across the United States, have been shaped by sprawling development. It will be quite a while before they reach any sort of smart growth ideal—if ever. But the people who live there still need to be able to reach their neighborhood schools safely and walk to and from the bus stop.

If I'm not focusing on the problem, or on the best solution, what on earth will I be talking about? It turns out that many communities are somewhere in the middle—grappling with current conditions as they make their way to creating better, safer streets. This book tells their stories and explores how they have made change happen. It examines what happens after a community has embraced a new vision but when the reality it faces is still a sprawling, automobile-dominated street network with a planning system geared to deliver more of the same. This book is about what such communities do next.

Acknowledgments

THIS BOOK DRAWS on the knowledge of many people about how to complete our streets. I wish I could name the hundreds of advocates, practitioners, elected officials, and others who helped inform the development of the ideas that drive the Complete Streets movement, but for practicality's sake I will restrict myself to those who gave of their time and insight in developing this book. Many people granted me interviews and patiently answered my follow-up questions; the names of some of them appear in the text, but I want to acknowledge the contributions of the rest. They include the following: Linda Bailey, Mitzi Baker, Jackie Boland, Michael Briggs, Charles Brown, Jack Broz, Dan Burden, Marissa Dolin, Jeff Dunkel, Marshall Elizer, Steve Elkins, James Gittemeier, Andy Hamilton, Cynthia Hoyle, Michael Huber, Nick Jackson, Dan Jatres, Mike Jelen, Deb Kingsland, James Lenker, Todd Litman, Sal Lopez, Jordana Maisel, Raymond McCormick, Leslie Meehan, Chris Morfas, Paul Morris, Michael Moule, Jill Mrotek Glenzinski, Chad Mullins, Randy Neufeld, Phil Pugliese, Karina Ricks, Kate Rube, James Shapard, Karin Tank, Ken Tatsuguchi, Jennifer Toole, Laura Torchio, Linda Tracy, Michael Weber, Bill Wilkinson, Jack Zabrowski, and Paul Zykofsky. I also drew on interviews conducted by Stephanie Potts and Christine Green for a National Complete Streets Coalition project, and I thank Coralette Hannon, Jana Lynott, Rene Ray, and Julia Fine for their support of projects that informed the content of this book.

I give special thanks to Stefanie Seskin, who helped me identify many of the stories told here, reviewed my text, and is responsible for much of the National Complete Streets Coalition's best work. She and the rest of the staff and steering committee of the Coalition deserve my heartfelt thanks for stepping up and successfully managing the Coalition's transition to new leadership so I would have the time and space to research and write. I particularly want to thank the following people for their participation in the transition, and for all the work they have done to advance the Complete Streets movement: Debra Alvarez, Geoff Anderson, Rich Bell, Roxanne Blackwell, Tim Blumenthal, David Carlson, Andy Clarke, Jeremy Grandstaff, Art Guzzetti, Michael Huber, Kit Keller, Roger Millar, Jeff Miller, Randy Neufeld, Margo Pedroso, Martha Roskowski, Darren Smith, Ron Thaniel, Catherine Vanderwaart, Tom von Schrader, Rich Weaver, Caron Whitaker, and Stacey Williams. I also want to acknowledge that in focusing on the implementation process, this book leaves out the stories of the advocacy organizations and thousands of volunteers who have been the primary force behind getting complete streets policies adopted in the first place. You know who you are, and I am grateful to you for your dedication to this vision.

The developers of Evernote software have earned my gratitude for helping me keep more than a thousand notes organized, and Roy Peter Clark held my hand virtually with his book *Writing Tools*. Many people stepped up and helped me find photographs for use in the book, most notably Scott Crawford, Andy Goretti, Dave Lustberg, Anne McMahon, and Martha Roskowski.

Douglas Stewart, Karina Ricks, and Rebecca Bright read the entire manuscript and provided valuable suggestions and support throughout the writing process. I also thank Susan Handy, Roy Kienitz, Debra Alvarez, Elizabeth Schilling, Randy Neufeld, and Stefanie Seskin for their insights on portions of the text. I thank my editor Heather Boyer of Island Press for her steadfast support and for pushing me toward greater clarity on each subsequent draft.

Finally, I want to thank my husband, Bob Bloomfield. Not only did he show great patience with this competitor for my time and attention, but he kept me sane with his insistence that even writers need to get out on bike rides and walks. Most importantly, he sustained me with his unwavering belief in this project and in me.

Portions of this text appeared in different forms in reports issued by the National Complete Streets Coalition and its partners, and in the Urban Design Journal.

A well-maintained four-lane road in the Midwest alongside a school
for children with disabilities. (Photo by Barbara McCann.)

Introduction

A S I WAS WORKING ON THIS BOOK, I took a break to make a presentation at a pedestrian safety meeting held at a branch of the Montgomery County Public Library in Germantown, Maryland, just north of Washington, DC. Two girls, children of one of the organizers, were eagerly passing around "pedestrian" gingerbread cookies, as about fifty people gathered on the cold winter afternoon. But despite the refreshments, attendees found little to celebrate. The meeting had been called soon after two residents, one a high school student, had been killed while walking in what is known as the "upcounty," the northern section of Montgomery County where decades of agriculture are giving way to spread-out, automobile-oriented development.

Much of the afternoon was spent discussing design solutions for an unmarked crosswalk on Stringtown Road, a new four-lane road designed to funnel interstate traffic to the new development in Clarksburg. A father begged for a marked crosswalk to help his children and other kids living in new homes reach Clarksburg Elementary School, which backed up to the new road. He brought photographs of women and children crossing at a T-intersection, marked only by curb cuts and a narrow median the county had installed when the road was built. County officials said a signal and a crosswalk must wait years, until completion of the cross street brings more traffic. They fear that simply painting a crosswalk will give the kids a false sense of security. One county official said she had good news for attendees: in the future, the County will stop installing curb cuts that raise expectations prematurely.

As attendees debated potential solutions, I couldn't help thinking that the issue was one of priorities. The school has been in this location since 1909. Planners should have been aware that children would move into the new homes built within sight of the school. If their safety had been given priority in the planning phase, the County could have left the traffic heading to Interstate 270 on its original route, on Clarksburg Road on the far side of the school. The new road could have been smaller, with fewer cars. If safe access had been prioritized during the design phase, the County could have incorporated a safe crossing while building the road. Now, the traffic-centered priorities that guided earlier decisions have made it much harder to achieve pedestrian safety: the needs of a dozen children are in direct conflict with the needs of hundreds of commuters—commuters who have no choice but to drive.

This story is repeated all across the United States. Go to a multilane road in a suburb in just about any state. One look tells you that people who are not in cars shouldn't be there. A second look tells you that they are—because they've tramped a visible trail in the grass. It probably won't be long before you spot people waiting by a bus stop or running across the street during a break in traffic. You might even see someone riding a bike, hugging the curb while passing drivers honk.

The Complete Streets movement arose to change the priorities of the transportation system that produced these roads. A broad coalition of bicycle riders, transportation practitioners, public health leaders, older Americans, smart growth advocates, real estate agents, and more came together to insist that we begin to build streets that are safe for everyone. We formed the National Complete Streets Coalition in the early 2000s to push for passage of complete streets policies. The policies—in the form of laws, resolutions, or internal agency directives—commit states, cities, and towns to building all future road projects to safely accommodate everyone using them. The movement took off: since 2005, more than half the states and close to five hundred local jurisdictions have adopted complete streets policies.[1] Many of the communities that have made this commitment are going on to study the long-standing gaps in their transportation network, rework their decision-making processes, write new guidance, and educate transportation professionals and citizens alike in the new approach to making transportation investments. From the state of North Carolina to the city of Chicago and from Edmonds, Washington, to Lee County, Florida, they are beginning to routinely build their roads differently: they integrate carefully engineered sidewalks, safer crossings, bicycle lanes, new types of intersections, traffic calming, and features that speed buses to their destinations.[2]

The Complete Streets movement has helped bring about a tremendous burst of activity and change in the way roads are planned, funded, designed, and built. But it is far from the first to point out that roads should be safe for everyone traveling along them, or to argue for more transportation choices. Road safety campaigns go back to the dawn of the automobile age; bicycle riders and transit boosters have been pushing for multimodal accommodation since the 1970s. More recently, this movement has been driven by changing American attitudes: a 2012 nationwide public opinion poll found that 63 percent of Americans would like to address traffic congestion by improving public transportation and designing communities for easier walking and bicycling.[3] America's supposed love affair with the car is giving way to a romance with smart phones, which are more easily operated on the bus or streetcar. In the United States and around the world, young people are delaying getting their licenses and are driving less. The growing ranks of older adults want greater access to public transportation. Indeed, demographic trends show a certain inevitability in the desire to transition to less car-dependent lifestyles.[4] More citizens and their elected officials are using bicycles, public transportation, and their feet to get around, and they are working for change.

The Complete Streets Change Model

These trends are helping fuel the Complete Streets movement. It also continues to spread because it brings something new to the table, but not what many people think. Sure, the catchy name is helpful. But beyond the name, the movement has found three keys to unlocking change in transportation practice—and none of them has much to do with safer road design. In brief, the strategies aim (1) to reframe the conversation about transportation in a simple and powerful way, (2) to build a broad base of political support for completing the streets, and (3) to provide a clear path to follow in transitioning to a multimodal process.

The lack of a design focus may surprise anyone who is following the explosion of exciting new street design guidelines, manuals, books, and individual projects that are getting deserved attention in transportation circles these days. A new design paradigm is clearly taking shape, one that envisions a more connected, inviting, and sustainable urban fabric. Much of the discussion in transportation circles surrounds more clearly defining this paradigm, arguing for shorter blocks, a clearer relationship between the street and the surrounding buildings, and innovative treatments that slow traffic and better protect pedestrians and people on bikes while giving priority to public transportation. Many people assume that the Complete Streets movement is just another voice in this chorus—for example, I've been asked many times to provide the ideal cross section for a complete street.

But defining the problem as a design issue—in a field already tightly bound by technical specifications—has obscured the other ingredients necessary to move a system fixated on providing for a single mode. Engineers and architects alike have been churning out innovative new design ideas for several decades, but they have only recently begun to gain traction. And in too many cities, tremendous effort has been put into promising new design solutions that have been applied to road projects a few times—and then have just sputtered and faded away.

The Complete Streets movement takes a step back and defines the problem differently. In our view, the primary problem is political and cultural. If transportation agencies are hewing to outdated design standards and still solving the problem of building roads for automobile speed and capacity, then the solution is for community leaders to be very clear that they now have a different problem for transportation professionals to solve. The day-to-day decisions made by practitioners may seem technical, but they are driven by an underlying political decision and by the priorities and values of the community. A complete streets policy initiative provides the clear direction to begin to change those decisions. The Complete Streets movement is succeeding not because it lays out a compelling design paradigm (it doesn't have one), but because it uses the three key strategies to help change the way transportation projects are chosen, planned, and built. Most of this book elaborates on how practitioners all over the country are successfully using these strategies to change their agencies, their roads, and their communities. Only by following these actions can places truly put new design ideas to use, persistently and consistently.

Map of the Book

This book tells a story of change and embeds tips, insights, and tools about the process of converting a community's transportation investments to ensure safe streets for everyone.

In chapter 1, I'll examine the factors that explain why the US transportation planning and construction system has been historically resistant to changing its singular focus on providing for automobile travel—as well as how those dynamics are now changing. Chapter 2 elaborates on how the Complete Streets movement approached this intractable system and found a way to change it, using the three key strategies. The chapter tells the story of the initial success of the Complete Streets movement in engaging thousands of people in the transportation policy process and giving reformers a new point of leverage.

But it turns out that adopting a policy is not even half of the effort required. The rest of the book is devoted to what happens after a policy has passed, and tells the stories of many professionals—planners, engineers, landscape architects, and others—who have brought policies from paper into practice.

This focus is necessary because in too many communities, after leaders or elected officials have adopted a policy, nothing happens. The exact nature of this gap between policy and implementation is the subject of chapter 3. In some places, practitioners don't view their jobs any differently, and roads go on being built as before. In others, tremendous effort goes into writing new street design standards, but they result in only minor changes to a few projects—a sidewalk here, a bike lane there. This chapter helps readers understand why communities get stuck—and goes on to explain why the best strategy for getting them unstuck involves reframing the way agencies view and approach the mission of making streets safe.

Lasting and fundamental change will come only if a policy inspires a transportation agency to reorient its work to fully and consistently consider the safety of all users. Changing the processes used inside agencies is the topic of chapter 4. The chapter divides the task into four steps to achieve full implementation: changing decision making, updating design guidance, providing training and education, and finding new ways to measure success. It tells the stories of planners, engineers, landscape architects, politicians, and other complete streets advocates who have successfully gotten beyond project-by-project battles to lead their agencies in changing their decision-making systems. The sum of their experiences begins to provide a clear path for others to follow in converting their own systems to complete streets.

Chapter 5 explores the many and varied opportunities to begin chang-ing systems to build complete streets. The application of these four steps will differ in communities of different sizes and types. At a large state agency, the challenge lies in getting the new approach down into the dis-tricts; in a city, it may be in getting departments to talk to each other. Growing cities will spend more time working with private developers, while older communities can focus their work on changing their current streets. Most of the chapter demonstrates that some of the most effective implementation strategies lie not in big capital improvement projects but in the most mundane repair projects and in the details of development codes. It explains the advantages of bringing about change not through big signature projects but through small, gradual improvements.

Many complete streets proponents have discovered that changing their institutions is not a straightforward fix. They realize that making the transformation requires political savvy, relationship-building skills, and inspired communication among practitioners, elected officials, residents, business leaders, and many other stakeholders—in short, the "building support" strategy of the Complete Streets movement. In chapter 6, prac-titioners tell stories of how they have used these skills to champion the complete streets concept, to build new alliances, and to change practice.

Complete streets proponents need tools to help them answer the most common but also the most loaded question about this initiative: how much will it cost? Chapter 7 provides four answers to this question, clari-fying that the first issue is dispelling many misconceptions about what a complete streets commitment will mean. It includes examples of some of the creative and convincing ways that jurisdictions have documented the larger benefits they are gaining by building streets for everyone.

Chapter 8 is also aimed at providing tools for those who now find themselves working every day to strike a new balance between automo-biles and other modes. This balance means setting new priorities in the allocation of space and resources. This chapter discusses the political and practical ramifications of those decisions and shares techniques that some communities are using to help them make those allocations in a fair way that helps meet broader community goals. The final chapter looks at how the Complete Streets movement intersects with other movements, and it asks whether the concept needs to be expanded in light of the rapid evolution of thinking about how we build sustainable communities for the next century.

This book uses many examples from places and people across the country that are intended to illustrate the principles discussed. These examples are not intended as prescriptions to follow or even necessarily as best practices. I return to the same places several times to help readers understand the variety of activities that are under way. Although the book does not include full case studies, you can find a list of such profiles in appendix A. That list includes places mentioned in the book as well as some of the many communities that informed the conclusions in this book but that I did not have the space to name. I'm sorry I was unable to write about every place taking an innovative approach (but that's a nice problem to have).

Some places pursuing complete streets are taking baby steps while others are striding toward a totally new approach—and there is something to learn at both ends of the spectrum. Most of the ideas I present are not visionary. We already have plenty of visionary thinking to tap. Instead, I am seeking to help practitioners and advocates move toward completing their streets, and I hope I have conveyed the process of discovery that I and others went through in unlocking the keys to change. In Rochester, Minnesota, and Seattle, Washington, the discovery came as practitioners read through every planning document they had—and then systematically realigned them all to a complete streets vision. In Salt Lake City, it was the revelation that the city could quickly install many miles of bike lanes—if they worked with the right department at the right time. For the State of New Jersey, it was realizing they needed to give engineers the permission to put down their manuals and look at every street in a new way. For me, it was listening to everyone's stories—and understanding the power of getting the right people in the room.

Complete streets policies won't instantly end needless pedestrian deaths or create multimodal nirvana. But over time, they will transform the systems that keep creating difficult safety problems like Stringtown Road. My hope is that this book will help jurisdictions take the idea of safe streets for all from paper into everyday practice.

Many roads in the United States are built for one purpose.
(Photo by Barbara McCann.)

CHAPTER ONE

Why We Build Incomplete Streets

THE FUNDAMENTAL PHILOSOPHY behind the Complete Streets movement can seem painfully obvious: roads should be safe for everyone traveling along them. But the history, political standing, habits, and orientation of the transportation industry in the United States have made it extraordinarily difficult for any policy movement to shift the way transportation projects are planned and built.

The United States is still living with the reverberations of the engineering triumph of the interstate highway system—a network of forty-seven thousand miles of limited-access freeways that knit the country together in the 1950s and 1960s.[1] Solving the design and safety challenges in creating this network set an orientation that persists to this day in US transportation planning, construction, and management.

That orientation is focused on solving problems by building roads that expanded the capacity for automobile travel. The interstate era did begin with a policy, the Federal Aid Highway Act of 1956. But the policy was driven by a project-focused vision: build a freeway network. The policy simply lined up all the systems to do so.

One of the first ways it did this was to turn this massive project over to the experts at the state departments of transportation (DOTs), and ever since, state highway departments have wielded considerable influence in Washington, DC, as well as in their own state capitals and small towns. They gained credibility with the spectacular success of the interstates they were building—and with the commonly held view that road building is a technical pursuit, best left to engineers. When engineers talk about how to relieve congestion and improve safety, elected officials still defer to their judgment. Their political independence has also been assured by how much money they control. At the federal level and in most states, gas taxes are dedicated to transportation, so the agencies have been insulated from the annual budgetary push and pull in the state legislature. The steady funding stream has also meant state and local departments could make a big difference in elected officials' districts, by filling potholes and delivering favored road projects. Road construction companies sometimes enjoy cozy relationships with agency leaders and top politicians.[2] State agencies also tend to exert outsized influence on the politically fractured Metropolitan Planning Organizations (MPOs) that help decide how federal transportation dollars will be spent in urban areas.

Transportation industry leaders grew used to steady support from politicians for the clearly stated mission of tackling pavement maintenance, traffic congestion, and motorist safety. For decades, politicians' most predictable role was participation in the annual ritual affirming the release of the Texas Transportation Institute's congestion rankings, particularly its calculation of the billions of dollars purportedly lost by Americans sitting in traffic. The politicians usually made vows to keep building roads to solve the problem.

The Modal Divide

Another factor at work is the habit of building projects that are specific to a single method of travel. The transportation sector regards each mode as a separate entity, requiring separate programming, funding, and facilities. Administrative structures and funding are almost always divided by mode. The federal structure in place today is a case in point and influences the organization of the state and local agencies that receive its money. The US Department of Transportation is largely defined by the separate modal agencies that were brought under its umbrella in 1967, including the Federal Highway Administration (FHWA) and Federal Transit Administration. They receive separate funding allocations and have separate policies—and are even under the jurisdiction of separate Senate committees. The nonmotorized modes—bicycling and walking—have not been important enough to rate their own administration or funding stream, but they maintain a clearly separate identity. The FHWA houses a small

Bicycle/Pedestrian Program, and designated bicycle/pedestrian coordinator positions are required in each state DOT.

Follow the money, and you'll find a long history of clearly separated federal funding streams for highways, transit, and other uses. Until recently, almost all federal surface transportation dollars came from the gas tax, with revenues growing right alongside the steady increase in the amount of driving. Highway proponents fought any "diversion" of these Highway Trust Fund revenues for uses that did not directly benefit motorists. And the "highway" money is structured in a way that ensures that investments focus on moving cars. In order to access federal dollars, every jurisdiction in the country must classify its roads by the "functional classification" system, which defines roads solely by the amount and type of traffic they carry and divides them into arterial (major) streets, collector streets, or local streets. This system sets up rigid expectations about how high a "Level of Service" should be provided on different road types—with high service defined as fast, free-flowing traffic. This requirement has proven a barrier to places that would like to more finely tune their road network to serve public transportation, nonmotorized users, and the residences and businesses alongside the road.

After gas tax revenues soared in the 1960s, 1970s, and 1980s, Congress made a policy change and transit began receiving about 20 percent of these funds starting in the 1980s. Transit dollars pay for buses and rail infrastructure (and a little bit for operations). Cities and advocates began to push for an even more diverse transportation infrastructure, and the federal transportation law passed in 1991 brought a measure of reform; its name was, after all, the Intermodal Surface Transportation Efficiency Act (commonly known as ISTEA, pronounced "iced tea"). Projects that served other needs were allowed access to the ever-growing pie of Highway Trust Fund revenues, although on a modest scale. Among other changes, the authorization set aside funding for projects that could help improve air quality, as well as a small set-aside for "Transportation Enhancements," with about half of those funds spent on bicycle or pedestrian projects.

But while ISTEA made changes to transportation funding that allowed a more multimodal approach, it didn't require any change in the systems created to deliver new roads or to maintain old ones. Most states were able to add new programs without disturbing decades of tradition and practice that treated highways, public transit, and nonmotorized transportation as entirely separate programs. The bill was reauthorized twice more under the same basic recipe: a bigger pie, but with the same flavor. The short-term bill passed in 2012, called MAP-21, also did little to challenge the separation of modes.

The extent of this separation can be seen in the varied funding programs that are brought together to finance a single transportation project. A state-administered highway interchange can use one funding source and ignore the presence of people on foot. A city may need to cobble together several funding sources to build one multimodal boulevard. The separation also occurs at the state and local levels. A jurisdiction may use bond measures for capital projects to increase automobile capacity; sales taxes, to fund public transportation; and special state funding programs dedicated to bicycle or pedestrian facilities. In many communities, sidewalk construction and maintenance is paid for by the owner of the abutting property.

The system of "silos" for transportation funding makes some sense

Curb ramp to nowhere in Jackson, Mississippi. (Photo by Judy McNeil.)

when the modes are airplanes or ships or when the facilities are freight rail or roads. But modal separation breaks down when it comes to bikes, feet, personal automobiles, and public transportation. People cannot be categorized neatly as cyclists, pedestrians, drivers, and transit users. Most people use more than one way to get around—even if the pedestrian portion of the trip is only a walk across a parking lot. In many cases, people switch from one mode to another midtrip, or use different modes in the course of a day. All four of these modes are part of a single network that allows people to meet daily personal transportation needs. Bicycling and walking serve as the "capillaries" of the transportation system, the small but essential connectors for trips that include driving or taking transit.

Transportation planning within modal silos has produced quite a number of spectacularly incomplete streets, particularly in suburban areas developed alongside the interstate system. Bicycle and pedestrian safety problems seem impossible to solve, because everyone assumes the solution is to find funding and space to build a separate multiuse path. The silos even extend to the type of pedestrian, as agencies trying to comply with the Americans with Disabilities Act install "curb ramps to nowhere" with no immediate plans to connect them with sidewalks.

These divisions reflect a system driven by projects and not policy. One of my colleagues used to refer to the federal transportation bill as a "policy free zone," designed to distribute road money to the states and little more. Reformers have tried again and again to pass policies to expand the universe of issues considered in transportation planning, but the system has proved surprisingly resistant to change: all the money and all the systems are geared toward putting road projects on the ground.

The public health community provides a model that crystalizes the problem and provides a road map to change. The Policy-Systems-Environmental (PSE) change model is now promoted by public health practitioners, including the Centers for Disease Control and Prevention, as central to their fight against the obesity epidemic. Under this model, lasting change in eating and activity patterns do not come about through the traditional campaigns aimed at changing individual behavior. Instead, they come about by changing the *policies* that influence the *systems* that create the *environments* that influence whether people eat well and are active.[3]

While the "PSE" theory posits that policies are the critical first phase in any change, transportation has had it upside down: the engine behind the industry starts with the environment, with road projects. The projects have driven the creation of systems for project delivery, and until recently, the policies have been no more than tweaks to help this project-driven system run better. This is one primary reason why change has come so hard to the transportation sector: policies simply have not driven the process.

Systems Designed for Mono-Modalism

With a clear project-driven mission, the surface transportation industry spent decades creating the systems that would help them deliver smooth, uncongested roads—and keep the ever-growing volume of traffic moving.[4] These systems have turned out to be a major barrier to creating a multimodal transportation network. Yet, since they are part of the inner workings of agencies, they have been largely out of the sight and reach of policy makers.

While these systems are numerous, a couple deserve elaboration. The most ubiquitous revolves around a tool used for measuring the success of transportation projects: automobile Level of Service (LOS). LOS calculates volume-to-capacity ratios for corridors and intersections and assigns a value-laden "A to F" score, with "A" meaning free-flowing traffic, and "F," a total backup. Many communities have made it a matter of policy or even statute to keep LOS from going below "C" or "D" at intersections, even at peak travel times. New transportation projects and new developments often have to predict and mitigate their impact on Level of Service. But by calculating only automobile delay at peak travel times, LOS has meant that commuter car trips are favored over every other potential use of a roadway.[5] It is often the *only* method used to rank and make decisions about projects—and it assumes that a community's primary goal is to minimize automobile delay. This gets in the way of providing more space for transit, allowing more compact development, or even letting people have enough time to walk across the street.

The most frequently cited system that stands in the way of complete streets is the heavy reliance on uniform road construction standards codified into design manuals. Under this traditional approach to transportation planning, the design manual is the be-all and end-all when it comes to making transportation decisions. The national design guide, issued by the Association of State Highway and Transportation Officials (AASHTO), is such a force that it simply goes by the (now somewhat ironic) name "The Green Book." Many states use its most conservative provisions as the basis for their own, formally adopted design standards. In many agencies, engineers follow the manuals scrupulously, using their state highway design manual and a suite of other manuals to look up specifications for every project.

Many an engineer worried about multimodal safety has pointed a finger at restrictive design standards. The engineers say their manuals won't allow the features needed to build roads that are safe for people on foot and bicycles, let alone do a better job of serving children, or older adults, or transit vehicles. And indeed, in many states, proponents of multimodal streets are constantly forced to seek "variances," or "design exceptions," to make space for transit patrons and people on foot or bicycle. This means they must exert a tremendous amount of effort for each project.

Systems inside the agencies are also built around a safety mission—but it, too, has had a narrow focus on preventing automobile crashes. Early safety studies were conducted in sparsely populated areas and concentrated on how to make the new, higher speeds of automobiles safer, mainly in the context of the new, controlled-access highways. They found that fewer crashes occurred on highways that were "forgiving" of driver error, so most guidance on safer streets recommended building roads with fewer things to crash into, with turns designed so they could be navigated at high speeds. As a result, the "design speed" of a roadway (for example, the highest safe speed to take a corner) would often be higher than the posted speed limit. And many jurisdictions have adopted policies that speed limits should be set according to the 85th percentile—the speed at which 85 percent of the drivers travel. These practices prioritized helping cars traveling at a high speed avoid crashes but did not address the effect of speed itself on anyone or anything they might crash into. And higher speeds lead to more serious injuries and fatalities. Pedestrians and bicyclists remain overrepresented in traffic fatalities, making up 15 percent of deaths in 2010 (injuries are not tracked on a national level).

If safety issues arise after a road is built to the standard specifications, a system of "warrants" guides many agencies in fixing them. This means they document crashes and use standardized thresholds for instituting safety measures when they become "warranted" by crash data. Planners and citizens committed to a vision for a multimodal future grind their teeth at agencies' insistence on counting crashes before so much as adding a crossing signal or redesigning a turn.

Even the academic institutions devoted to transportation research kept a narrow, project-oriented focus: for many years, research concentrated on seeking the best formula for hot-mix asphalt or creating quantitative models to predict and measure traffic volumes. For decades, traffic grew so steadily that the question was never whether it would grow but always where, and how much. Traffic models continued to assume that almost all trips would be by private automobile; data was not even collected on the number of people walking, riding bicycles, or taking transit. Little research explored how to manage travel demand by using a mix of modes or land use patterns. Despite the common wisdom of the popular phrase "build it and they will come," studies confirming the phenomenon of "induced demand" remained outside of mainstream transportation thinking. This research challenges the effectiveness of relieving congestion with increased capacity, because it shows that new roads induce additional travel. Happily, transportation research has broadened considerably in the last fifteen years, but bringing new results to the attention of practitioners remains a slow process.

The Cultural Divide

The people who work inside these modally organized structures and systems tend to be divided as well. When I talk to complete streets proponents about how it's going, often at some point someone leans in, lowering his or her voice to say, "There's an engineer here who just doesn't get it. He blocks everything we try to do." The person may joke that the best course of action is an early retirement program.

Many complete streets efforts are led by planners or landscape architects, whose training predisposes them to the movement's inclusive, policy-driven approach; engineers are more likely to stick with thinking of their work in terms of delivering projects according to clearly defined standards.

John LaPlante, a traffic engineer who is also a leading voice on complete streets, acknowledges the cultural divide. He says: "People become planners for different reasons than they become engineers. Engineers are uncomfortable with the touchy-feely, feel-good stuff. Engineers really like certainty." LaPlante may stand out a bit in engineering circles with his goatee and direct sense of humor, but he has worked since the late 1980s to change transportation engineering from the inside—by changing its design manuals, and more importantly, how these are used.

LaPlante would argue that a bigger obstacle than the design manuals themselves is the "cookbook" approach to their use. LaPlante is quick to point out that the Green Book allows narrower automobile lanes and other design elements that help create complete streets, and that the book itself makes clear that the numbers it contains are guidelines—not hard and fast standards. But LaPlante says some engineers are reluctant to use their engineering judgment. He notes that when teaching a complete streets training course to engineers in Massachusetts, he discussed the need to weigh the merits of various options for accommodating different road users. "Some really objected. They were upset with not having a table [of specifications] to go to. I tried to tell them, 'that's why you go to school, to learn engineering judgment. If you are just going to take a number out of a table, all we need is to do is hire someone who has learned how to read!'" A cookbook approach precludes the trade-offs and judgments that need to be made when coming up with design solutions that serve automobiles, public transportation, trucks, bicycles, and pedestrians of all ages and abilities. LaPlante partially blames the legal system for fostering this attitude among engineers; lawyers filing lawsuits have used deviation from guidance against transportation agencies.

But the bias remains. Often when planners or urban designers want to provide more space for pedestrians or bicycles or trees, they draw up the concept and hand it off to engineers for final design—who then align the project with engineering standards, unraveling the multimodal intent. For example, a tight turn, intended to slow cars, might be softened; a proposed landscaped median might become a narrow ribbon median in order to maintain a standard twelve-foot traffic lane.

Other practitioners confirm the cultural divide and note that it isn't all about personalities. Part of what is happening is that planners are making decisions on projects that public works engineers will have to build—and then maintain. The cultural divide is exacerbated in the structural divide between planning and construction. Transportation planning is typically in a separate division or department from public works, which is responsible for constructing and maintaining the roads. So a fundamental tension arises when the planning department is setting policy that has an impact on the budget and activities of public works: the engineers are often justifiably concerned that new infrastructure will lead to new expectations and new maintenance demands.

Forces Converging to Ease Change

All of these forces—funding and systems oriented toward project delivery and divided by modes, the political independence of agencies, and the divisions among personnel—work against opening up transportation planning to a more diverse and policy-driven orientation. But in many places, the headwind of traditional practice that complete streets proponents have faced has been easing for some time.

Broader trends are forcing transportation agencies to be more open to complete streets and other reforms. After decades of steady to explosive growth, the total miles driven per capita peaked in mid-2005 and has been falling since. Car travel continued to drop for seven years despite an improving economy and a stabilization of gas prices.[6] This decline in driving, and the advent of more fuel-efficient vehicles, has led to falling gas tax revenues—and has completely upended the politics of transportation budgeting. Attempts to raise the federal gas tax have gone nowhere. The arguments that worked in the past to keep the money flowing, such as a need to build roads to ease congestion, are not working so well. A growing number of communities and states have realized that they can no longer afford massive highway projects, and that the billions spent on preventing delay have not delivered; people want new solutions. In short, the transportation industry is being forced to become more responsive to the political process, and to the policies that it produces.

With the bottom dropping out of the project-driven transportation sector, policies are finally starting to assert some influence. This shift provides an opening for the Complete Streets movement, with a change model that holds that political leaders must set down a clear and simple policy directive to make the streets safe for everyone; agencies must then change the systems they use to make decisions on all upcoming road projects, and this is what will ultimately result in a changed environment and more complete streets. These three phases of change fit neatly with the Policy-Systems-Environmental change model of the public health movement.

The opportunity for policy to begin to drive change applies to goals beyond complete streets; big cities in particular are adopting policies to make limited transportation investments serve multiple goals, including driving economic development, lowering greenhouse gas emissions, and providing healthier travel alternatives.

The modal divide remains firmly in place in federal and state law, spending, and bureaucracies, but the US DOT has taken many steps to soften the boundaries, through spending programs, guidance, and cross communication. As documented by the State Smart Transportation Initiative, many state DOTs are becoming more innovative as well, increasing efficiency, changing their internal processes, and paying more attention to transportation options.[7]

A sea change is also under way in the design manuals. LaPlante is partially responsible, as he helped write the first bicycle guide as a companion to the Green Book in the late 1990s, using an unprecedented process that engaged a broad variety of practitioners. The book is a best seller; pedestrian guidelines followed, and a separate process under the ADA has resulted in the creation of disability design guidelines targeted specifically for streets. LaPlante lists changes to other manuals as well—the Highway Capacity Manual, and the Manual of Uniform Traffic Control Devices, and the Green Book itself. New research that supports a more multimodal approach to safety is starting to work its way into these official tomes. But will engineers still try to use these guides as "cookbooks" to follow? LaPlante is optimistic. "The cookbook now doesn't say use a cup of flour and a pinch of salt," he says. "It says taste it, look at it, see how it works. It grants flexibility." And many engineers, who are problem solvers at heart, are embracing the new set of problems they are being given.

These positive trends lay the groundwork. But the complex task of transforming one-size-fits-all automobile-oriented transportation planning into a flexible, multimodal system has a long way to go. The Complete Streets movement presents one model for cutting through the barriers, pointing to the current condition of roads across the country to say, everyone using these roads should be safe.

Advocates in Honolulu, led by AARP volunteers, work to build support
for an upcoming vote on a county complete streets policy. It passed.
(Photo by Jackie Boland.)

CHAPTER TWO

How the Complete Streets Movement Succeeds

M ANY PEOPLE AND PUBLICATIONS have introduced the complete streets concept by defining a complete street as a roadway that is designed and operated for the safety of everyone using it—whether by car or bike, foot or bus. This appealing definition tells only part of the story: the Complete Streets movement is at its heart a policy initiative that seeks to change the way *all* roads are built in the United States. The movement's success is rooted not in the simple definition of a complete street but in three key strategies aimed at changing transportation practice. These strategies focus on shifting a discussion centered on project design to instead address values and policy, building a broad base of support for policy change, and, finally, creating a clear path to transform everyday practice.

This chapter cites social science research that informed the development of the movement's strategies, but their development owes far more to the contributions made by the many people who helped form the National Complete Streets Coalition. Their sophisticated understanding of the public policy process and of transportation practice helped craft an initiative that would be widely accepted and would spark a lasting change to the way roads are planned and built in towns, cities, and states across the country. The movement has unlocked an intransigent transportation planning and construction system by asserting a new, more inclusive view of transportation; by developing a clear path from current practice toward a multimodal future; and by recognizing that successfully negotiating this path requires not only technical savvy but an understanding of political processes and the building of support and new alliances.

Spreading the Word: A New Frame

The name *Complete Streets* came out of an effort to help bicycle advocates get past a technical term that was holding them back on Capitol Hill. They wanted to include a directive in federal law that bicycle facilities should be a routine part of planning for all road projects. But the term they were using for this directive, "Routine Accommodation Policy," wasn't exactly grabbing attention—and it sounded like one of those technicalities best left to the transportation experts. Martha Roskowski, then manager of the federal advocacy coalition America Bikes, asked me, as media manager, to come up with a new name. In late 2003, I convened a series of brainstorming sessions and invited some of the best minds I knew who worked on communications in transportation, including David Goldberg of Smart Growth America. Over three sessions, we discussed many names and at some point David suggested "complete streets." We conducted our own informal market testing with friends and neighbors, and gradually I realized that this was more than a new name—it might be a way to reframe the discussion about transportation to include everyone using the roads. I had followed the work of George Lakoff, the Berkeley linguist who has written extensively about the power of metaphors in the political arena. He became well-known for his discussion of the power of creating a new "frame" for an issue. The framing of "complete streets" may be most powerful in its implicit definition of its opposite. No one wants to build incomplete streets.

This was the first of the insights that emerged to help transform complete streets from a phrase used in a few inside-the-beltway policy documents to a genuine movement taken up by bicycle advocates and public health officials, mayors and transportation commissioners, local senior organizations and newspaper editorial boards.

While complete streets can be dismissed as a cute phrase, it represents a radically new view of transportation infrastructure—at least for the transportation industry. As discussed in chapter 1, transportation planning, funding, and design have always been separated by modes. A complete streets approach requires transportation agencies to see the potential for all roads, and for all road projects and funding streams, to contribute to the goal of safely serving people whether they are driving their own cars, riding a bus, or using a bicycle or their feet. It clarifies that the roads must be safe for a variety of people, including older adults, children on their way to school, and people with disabilities. The degree of the conceptual leap required is revealed when transportation professionals and policy makers try to fit the phrase into their framework of transportation silos, talking about "complete streets elements," and using the term as a synonym for the bicycle and pedestrian features of a roadway. This usage perpetuates the separation of modes; in many cases, those using this terminology also assume that special funding is required to add these "amenities" to the road. In fact, complete streets require a holistic look at how a street serves everyone using it—including drivers.

By reframing the transportation safety problem to include all people traveling along a corridor, the problem itself shifts. As many as one third of the population in the United States does not drive: children, older adults, people with disabilities, and those without the financial resources to own a car. The focus must expand from the vehicle lanes to include the adjoining "goat trail" tramped by pedestrians—forcing the acknowledgment that people who are not in cars are already using the roadway. In this way, an existing safety problem becomes both more urgent and visible— and clearly the responsibility of the transportation sector.

The Complete Streets movement widens the focus even further, moving out from the individual road corridor to a jurisdiction's entire network. It calls not for building individual complete streets but for adopting federal, state, and local complete streets policies. A majority of the policies adopted across the country are resolutions passed by city councils, but dozens of cities and counties have adopted local ordinances and their agencies have written their own internal policies; a few policies have started out as executive orders. At the state level, legislatures have passed laws, and DOTs have adopted formal internal directives. What all the policies have in common is a simple declaration that all future projects undertaken by a transportation agency will accommodate all users of the roadway.[1] The policy may list these users, including people of all ages and abilities who are walking, riding bicycles, and catching public transportation, as well as covering operators of public transportation vehicles, automobiles, and freight. This policy solution has helped hundreds of communities break out of a frustrating focus on individual technical fixes and take on the task of building support for changing an entrenched transportation paradigm.

The policy focus also puts fundamental transportation decision making firmly into the wheelhouse of elected officials. This has several ramifications, but in terms of reframing it gives an edge to a movement seeking to address transportation issues in a new way. Politicians are particularly good at articulating visions that help their community reframe an issue. It is powerful when a city alderman says, "I want to ensure that we design our streets to be safe, enhance quality of life, and allow people to travel freely regardless of whether they walk, bike, take transit, or drive."[2] When St. Louis alderman Shane Cohn said this upon passage of a city complete streets bill, it carried weight—and it set a new standard for how the city would approach street design.

This simple and powerful vision stands in stark contrast to the complexity of many earlier attempts to turn around a transportation industry driven more by projects than by policy. Take, for example, reforms instituted in 1991 through the federal legislation ISTEA. The legislation inserted policies that tried to broaden the mission of the transportation industry, introducing fifteen "planning factors" that regions using federal funding had to consider (states got twenty-three), such as "the overall social, economic, energy, and environmental effects of transportation decisions" (and that's a single factor).[3] But the planning factors were as vague and ambitious as the existing agency practices were specific and targeted. No one provided a way to apply these new policy goals in a system geared to building roads to solve the simple and vital problem of traffic congestion. Over time, it became clear that people inside the agencies were simply checking off boxes, indicating they had "considered" these detailed and complex planning factors. While the complete streets concept requires a conceptual shift, the policies don't ask for the moon; they merely put transportation agencies and their employees on notice that they are responsible for the safety of everyone using the road.

To the general public, the concept seems so simple that it can have a "duh" quality. Of course roads should be safe for everyone; dozens of newspaper editorial boards have said as much in articulate pieces that were an early boost to the movement. But it provides a powerful rejoinder to complaints that safety proposals will impede traffic, succinctly challenging the assumption that the movement of automobiles always takes priority. It raises awareness of road design as a factor in pedestrian crashes, which are still too often blamed on the actions of the victim.

The name has limits. When used consistently as shorthand for "bicycle/pedestrian infrastructure," or as a rallying cry by a narrow constituency, it can take on a negative taint. People in a few communities have found it doesn't work for them. But many strong policies never use the term. The name itself is far less important than pushing for a new approach to transportation planning, one that takes the safety of all users into account.

The complete streets concept brings a simple and unified vision to a field that has been divided by funding, standards, and details. But back when the term was first coined, the leadership at America Bikes knew that reframing alone would not be enough to advance the concept. We needed to build broad support and to make clear the next actions that would help achieve it.

Building the Coalition: Gathering Political Support

It turned out that it wasn't too hard to find supporters. The Complete Streets movement was started by bicycle advocates but was quickly taken up and advanced by people working in public health, activists for older adults, proponents of smart growth, public transportation agencies, disability advocates, and even real estate agents. All of these groups can make persuasive arguments about why they want a more diverse street environment. Bicycle and pedestrian advocates want safer streets that will encourage more people to walk and ride. Public health officials, driven by the obesity crisis, point to research that shows that people who live in places with sidewalks, bike lanes, and safe bus stops get more daily physical activity. Older adults want to be able to "age in place," which means designing streets to be safer for older drivers to navigate and for older pedestrians who may need more time to cross the street safely. Smart growth advocates see complete streets as an essential element in changing communities to be more compact and more sustainable. Public transportation agencies use the streets to move a high volume of people and are starting to push for a higher priority for their vehicles and passengers. Advocates for disabled people are tired of disconnected curb ramps and a lack of audible signals. Real estate agents have come to understand that the higher-quality street environments brought by complete streets raise and sustain home values. And transportation professionals who want better outcomes are also speaking up, via professional associations representing engineers, planners, bicycle and pedestrian professionals, and landscape architects.

The wide variety of constituents speaking on one issue moves elected officials to act. In Spokane, Washington, city council member Jon Snyder, who had championed a policy for the city, described the dramatic council meeting at which the policy was approved: "A lot of the testimony last night focused on the health and safety aspects of Complete Streets. We heard from disabled veterans, folks from Lighthouse for the Blind, grade school teachers, physicians, neighborhood representatives, and small business owners imploring us to help make our streets safer for all users and to address the epidemics of obesity and diabetes that result from inactivity. In all, more than forty people testified and [the state land use advocacy group] Futurewise turned in a petition with an additional 500 names in support."[4]

The original vision statement of the National Complete Streets Coalition reads:

"**Complete streets are designed and operated to enable safe access for all users.** Pedestrians, bicyclists, motorists and transit riders of all ages and abilities must be able to safely move along and across a complete street. Creating complete streets means changing the policies and practices of transportation agencies. **A complete streets policy ensures that the entire right of way is routinely designed and operated to enable safe access for all users.** Transportation agencies must ensure that all road projects result in a complete street appropriate to local context and needs" [emphasis in original].

That 2011 city council meeting was one local outcome of a coalition-building strategy that started years earlier at the national level. It started when I invited groups to join a task force to get a complete streets measure into the federal transportation bill. After the bill passed in 2005 without a complete streets provision, the task force became the National Complete Streets Coalition. We agreed on a definition of the term *complete streets* and set a goal of spreading policies not just at the federal level but in states and localities: our first target was to achieve policies in five states and twenty-five cities.

The Coalition is steered by a committee that includes bicycle and pedestrian advocacy groups (e.g., America Bikes), public interest groups (e.g., AARP and the American Public Transportation Association), practitioner organizations (e.g., the Institute of Transportation Engineers, the American Planning Association, and the American Society of Landscape Architects), and public health groups (e.g., Active Living by Design, Blue Cross/Blue Shield of Minnesota), as well as the National Association of Realtors. Smart Growth America, a group that supports more sustainable planning, hosted the Coalition in the early years (and now staffs it as one of its programs).[5] Consulting firms that offer multimodal planning and design services are also important supporters of the Coalition, and groups as diverse as the YMCA and the Natural Resources Defense Council have worked to advance the complete streets concept.

From the beginning, this was not just a letterhead coalition. Member groups of the steering committee, the bicycle industry association Bikes Belong, consulting firms, and other interest groups made financial commitments for the coordinating work, participated in clarifying the vision, and launched and staffed their own complete streets research and advocacy projects. This was not some new, separate organization they were supporting; it was a concept that each fully owned and embraced. Under the advice of Randy Neufeld, the founder of the Chicago Active Transportation Alliance and one of the strategic minds behind the national bicycle movement, I kept organizational structure to a minimum so we could focus on spreading the concept. The Coalition's purposefully loose structure encouraged the widest possible ownership, and it showed in the variety of products and initiatives it started to produce. AARP launched the first major research project to develop a complete streets manual, *Planning Complete Streets for an Aging America*. The American Planning Association issued a Planners Advisory Service report on complete streets best practices. The Association of Bicycle and Pedestrian Professionals worked with me to develop a workshop program and find and train instructors to provide it.

I was a student of Everett Rogers's diffusion innovation theory, which holds that the development of a highly effective diffusion network is essential to the transmission of a new idea or practice.[6] Rogers's diffusion model stresses the importance of peer networks and champions; the closer the champions are to the targeted adopters, the more effective they will be. On our shoestring budget, the Coalition pursued a strategy that depended on each member using its own communications networks to promote the benefits of complete streets. Each group, from AARP to YMCA, reached out to its constituency and engaged its strengths in working for policy adoption at the federal, state, and local levels. The strong relationships between the messengers and those receiving the message meant speedy dissemination. The complete streets concept has spread so quickly and thoroughly in part because so many people first heard about it from peers they respect.

As the diverse national Coalition members wrote reports and articles and made presentations at their conferences, their state and local affiliates turned to leading policy adoption campaigns. AARP joined up with health and bicycle groups in Hawaii and got to work on one of the first legislative campaigns, and then followed it with more in several states; bicycle advocates launched one in Illinois. In some smaller jurisdictions, such as Colorado Springs, Colorado, transportation professionals helped add complete streets provisions to master and strategic plans. The health insurance firm Blue Cross/Blue Shield of Minnesota added complete streets policies to their active living initiative, working with local transportation professionals toward policy adoption; their efforts culminated in a successful state legislative campaign led by a local environmental group, Fresh Energy. YMCA worked on policy campaigns as part of its Pioneering Healthy Communities initiative; the Safe Routes to School National Partnership made the passage of complete streets policy a fundamental part of its strategy.

All of this activity meant that the Coalition soon surpassed its early target of five state and twenty-five local policies. You could theorize that the complete streets concept took off because it clearly defined a problem, identified a good solution, and was therefore adopted—that would be a rational view of the public policy process. But public policy researchers have found that this is not how change happens. Policy making is essentially a political battle over what values will prevail, and ultimately over the allocation of public resources.[7] Complete streets policy initiatives

AARP volunteers conduct a walking audit during Complete Streets Week
in New York in 2010; the New York state legislature passed a complete streets
law the following year. (Photo courtesy William Stoner.)

make that discussion of values explicit, but more importantly, they build
strong coalitions—essentially political power—to support what is in the
end a cultural and institutional change.

The need to build a network of support extends into the transportation agencies and the transportation profession. The policies give support to the practitioners who are already trying to change old ways from
within—they need the backing of their leaders as they upend tradition
and create new ways of doing business. They need the clarity of the policy to help the community to understand, affirm, and support the new
approach. This is why the Complete Streets movement has been taken
up with such enthusiasm not only by the advocacy interests but also by
planners, engineers, landscape architects, public works directors, and the
myriad of professionals involved in transportation planning.

Getting It Right: A Clear Path

Malcolm Gladwell's book about how change happens, *The Tipping Point*,
says that for a change to succeed, it must be "sticky": it must be memorable

(read: simple), and it must be actionable.[8] The complete streets concept is simple and memorable. But what does Gladwell mean by "actionable"? His book includes an account of a well-known study by Howard Levanthal that found the key to persuading college seniors to get a tetanus shot was not a compelling or graphic account of the consequences of the disease; rates of vaccination remained at the same low level (3 percent) whether students received factual information or heard graphic stories about the ravages of tetanus. The key to changing vaccination rates was unrelated to tetanus itself. In each group, some students also got a map showing where the health center was located on campus and its hours. As Gladwell points out, these were seniors who surely knew where the health center was. Yet the rate of vaccination among those who received the maps shot up to 28 percent. What the map did was help them relate the information about tetanus to their own lives so they could visualize themselves taking action.

Shifting to a multimodal transportation system is far more complicated than getting a tetanus shot, but those who want to achieve it still need a map. The Complete Streets movement provides a clear guide to help communities make the shift. Once advocates or practitioners are clear that they want complete streets, their first action is the writing and passage of a clear multimodal policy commitment, informed by the vision of the community. In the second phase, the focus is on the process of changing the systems, culture, and practices inside of transportation agencies so they can begin to build streets that are safe for all users. The technicalities of building the streets themselves come only as part of the third phase: building projects.[9]

The Coalition has focused on developing resources to guide advocates and practitioners in the first two phases of the transformation. When it first formed, the Complete Streets Task Force worked on developing a policy for the next federal transportation authorization that would ensure that all future road projects receiving federal dollars would take into account the needs of all road users, and we rooted it in existing policy documents. The FHWA had written a clear bicycle and pedestrian accommodation policy in 2000 that called for establishing "bicycle and pedestrian ways" in new construction and reconstruction projects in urbanized areas.[10] I uncovered about a dozen examples of "proto-complete streets" policies, including Oregon's 1971 "Bike Bill," San Francisco's "Transit First" policy, and the "routine accommodation" policy passed by the regional planning commission for Columbus, Ohio; several states had also adapted the FHWA guidance.[11]

The initial research into proto-complete streets policies to inform federal action expanded and became a guide for state and local jurisdictions that wanted to make their own policy commitment ensuring that transportation projects take into account the needs of all users. The research was disseminated by task force member the Alliance for Biking and Walking, and this was the beginning of a core technique for the (then future) Coalition: learning from innovative places and practitioners around the country. Over time, the Coalition created a checklist of ten elements that help a complete streets policy succeed. The National Complete Streets Coalition now keeps track of policy adoption, sharing success stories and recognizing those who adopt. It provides accessible resources on what constitutes a good policy, issuing annual reports ranking the strength of policies as well creating other resources to help communities write their own policies.[12] These activities support transportation agency leaders who have a strong desire to excel among their peers, and the resources developed provide guidance to the Coalition's diverse set of champions as they promote new policies and implementation campaigns without personal intervention from the small Coalition staff. This created the conditions that allowed extensive independent policy adoption activity to bubble up quickly. All of the policy information from around the country has also come back to inform the Coalition's continued work to include a complete streets provision in federal transportation law, via several versions of the Safe and Complete Streets Act, introduced into both houses of Congress starting in 2008.

The Coalition also paid close attention to the second phase of the conversion to complete streets: institutionalizing change inside of transportation agencies. The Coalition staff and partners collected and disseminated field research on the implementation process; much of this research informs the content of this book. The Coalition has been working on creating an implementation standard that will provide a clear view of what to do next, and that will reward the communities that are leading the way.

The third phase, construction of projects, is being taken care of by the dozens of new design manuals and books that make clear the many options for building multimodal roadways. Indeed, many books and blogs go even further, making a valuable contribution by grappling with solutions to the long-neglected interface between buildings, people, and the street. The Coalition shares information about design questions and includes design issues in its workshops, but frankly, project-oriented solutions are already getting plenty of attention from others. The Coalition remains focused on policy adoption and implementation.

Complete Streets Gains Traction . . . and Shows Results

Many transportation professionals and citizens have been trying to solve the problem of incomplete streets for decades on a project-by-project basis, suggesting new street designs, fighting for inclusion of bicycle paths and sidewalks, and finding funding and support to build a few beautiful boulevards. The National Complete Streets Coalition's change model has given this work traction. The movement has been successful in reframing a critical piece of the transportation puzzle in part because the frame itself is memorable—sticky, as Malcolm Gladwell would say—and because it offered a clear path for taking action and building the network of relationships necessary for rapid dissemination.[13] At steering committee meetings, Coalition members seemed to embrace my slightly quirky titles for the programs we launched together implementing these three strategies: "Spreading the Word," "Building the Coalition," and "Getting It Right."

With minimal Coalition structure and staff, Complete Streets policy adoption rose, and then soared. Fewer than a dozen proto-policies existed prior to 2003; in 2006, fifteen jurisdictions adopted new policies. In 2010, eighty-five jurisdictions adopted new policies; in 2011, 140 new policies were added to the list. By the time this book reaches print, well over five hundred policies will be in place in the United States. In early 2013, policy adoption was reported from Memphis, Tennessee, to the Las Vegas, Nevada, region and from Maplewood, Minnesota, to Manatee County, Florida. Twenty-seven states, the District of Columbia, and Puerto Rico have adopted policies, and a number of Canadian cities and provinces have as well.[14] When we started, I kept a file of each time I saw the term *complete streets* appear in print—and I would forward each article to the steering committee. That became impossible long ago—and even tracking policy adoption has become a burden for the Coalition's small staff. As I hope is made clear throughout this book, thousands of people have taken up the complete streets approach and made it their own.

Some places are already demonstrating the benefits of orienting their work toward safer streets. Cities using a complete streets approach are seeing lower crash numbers on specific streets as well as citywide. Seattle installed new crossings and bus plazas and redesigned busy Aurora Avenue; total crashes dropped by 21 percent. A reconfiguration on Nickerson Street showed similar results and reduced speeding by "top-end speeders" (those going ten or more miles over the speed limit) by 90 percent.[15] New York City reports injury reductions of up to 67 percent from dozens of new treatments that narrow automobile lanes and add bicycle lanes, medians, and safety islands.[16] The city reports a 37 percent reduction in traffic fatalities in the last decade, with deaths in 2009 dropping to their lowest level in a century. Note that most of these statistics indicate safety improvements are in store for *all* traffic crashes—not just for people on foot and bicycle.

Safer streets are making possible the other goals that advocates want streets to deliver, from improved health to sustainability to economic vitality.

Public health advocates have been a primary supporter of the Complete Streets movement; they want to get more people out on foot and bicycle so they can reach the minimum requirement of thirty minutes a day of moderate physical activity. But a lack of safe places to walk and fear of traffic are a big barrier—for most people, getting hit by a car is a bigger immediate health threat than eventual diabetes or heart disease. But the potential is enormous: the last National Household Transportation Survey showed 41 percent of all trips in the United States are less than three miles, an easy distance to walk or ride a bike or bus. Sixty-seven percent of those trips are now taken in a car.[17]

Walkable streets can change that. Multiple studies have shown that creating a safer street environment with sidewalks, bike lanes, redesigned crossings, and the like results in higher rates of walking and bicycling.[18] Many places discussed in this book are proof of this; for example, in Nashville, Tennessee, the city has grown its bicycle network from seven

A traffic circle on La Jolla Boulevard in San Diego, shortly after construction.
(Photo by Dan Burden.)

miles to over one hundred miles, and has documented that the number
of people bicycling shot up 50 percent between 2009 and 2011. The city
is enhancing its transit stops, sidewalks, and crosswalks as well. Another
set of studies shows that people getting around by bike, foot, and transit
have lower obesity rates and chronic disease.[19] No wonder the Centers
for Disease Control and Prevention lists complete streets as an effective
anti-obesity strategy.

Getting more people out walking, bicycling, and taking public transportation means fewer car trips, and that means less greenhouse gas emissions. International climate scientists at the Intergovernmental Panel on
Climate Change recommend shifting modes as a key long-term strategy
to mitigate the disruptions that are resulting from climate change. Again,
studies show that providing better facilities results in more people leaving
their cars behind. A study issued by the Washington State DOT found that
filling in a community's sidewalk network so that 70 percent of streets
offer safe pedestrian space reduces vehicular travel by 3.4 percent and carbon emissions by 4.9 percent.[20] Changes to streets that speed buses can
also result in a shift that reduces carbon emissions: people flocked to Los
Angeles's first Rapid Bus service; ridership shot up 30 to 40 percent, with

one third of the patrons being new riders who had never used public transportation—and who were likely leaving their own automobiles behind.[21]

A new transportation paradigm is likely to deliver both environmental and health benefits, but its realization will depend on completing streets for the safety of all users. A study of the impact of "active transportation" on the San Francisco Bay Area finds that its potential to cut carbon emissions rivals the reductions possible through greater use of low-emission vehicles. The same study finds that the predicted increase in physical activity would deliver a reduction in cardiovascular disease risk "rank[ing] among the most notable public health achievements in the modern era." But the study, published in the *American Journal of Public Health*, also predicts a substantial increase in traffic injuries to bicyclists and pedestrians and so calls for a focus on creating safer streets.[22]

Many cities and towns are pursuing complete streets policies for a much more immediate, localized goal: bringing economic vitality to their communities. Some of the most innovative cities working for complete streets, such as Chicago and Washington, DC, see complete streets as a primary part of a broader strategy to stoke their economic engines by creating compact, walkable places. The San Diego region and city were early adopters of a complete streets approach, and the city documented the economic value of an extensive redesign of La Jolla Boulevard in the business district known as Bird Rock by surveying tax receipts from the ninety-five businesses along the corridor. They showed a 20 percent boost in sales after the city installed traffic circles, safety features, and landscaping. The strategy is not limited to big cities; small towns from Montclair, New Jersey, to Tupelo, Mississippi, see complete streets as essential to rebuilding main streets and attracting and retaining workers. As discussed in more detail in chapter 7, New York and other places are documenting the benefits of complete streets in terms of dollars and cents.

These examples of successes are from places that have taken the principle of complete streets and put it into daily practice. But even with the movement's initial success, policy adoption is too often no more than an empty promise. After an initial policy victory comes the most important question: "Now what?"

Complete streets policies should end disconnects like this one.
(Photo by Judy McNeil.)

CHAPTER THREE

Closing the Gap between Policy and Practice

C ITY COUNCIL MEMBERS may consider a complete streets policy proposal during a hearing in their oak-paneled council chamber, as they sit in a row at their curved dais.. Residents may line up to speak into microphones about the safety of their children on the way to school and the grandmother who has trouble crossing the street. Others may express concern about the cost of new facilities or traffic congestion. Planners and engineers from the city staff may be called upon to deliver a PowerPoint presentation; they may contrast photos of barren, car-filled streetscapes with images of inviting, leafy green boulevards filled with people on foot and bicycle. The vote may be dramatic and close, with a raising of hands; it may be no more than a clerk reading off the measure, quick unanimous ayes, and a final gavel. Local TV, newspapers, and blogs will report on the community's new commitment to ensuring that future street projects are built to be safe for everyone. Advocates will cheer and celebrate, seeing the payoff from months of fact finding and coalition building.

But the next phase usually begins out of sight, back in the planning and public works departments, in offices with unremarkable desks cluttered with maps, project development forms, citizen complaint letters, and design directives from the state. The staff may gather in worn chairs in a windowless conference room to contemplate how they can turn this lofty goal into day-to-day practice. Or, they might just keep doing their jobs as before, leaving the gap between vision and reality untouched.

While adoption of a complete streets policy is the first step on a clear path for changing transportation practice, the attempt to marshal political and community support behind a new approach to transportation planning too often flounders once the policy is in place. This is particularly true when the effort has been made primarily from the outside, when advocates or lawmakers have created and adopted a policy with resistance or only lukewarm interest from the transportation agency that has to implement it. The advocates' euphoria may wear off quickly, when absolutely nothing happens inside the department after the policy passes. Or the disillusionment may come more slowly, after many months of working with the agency's staff and leadership only to find that the changes made are minor or have been blocked by midlevel management.

The advocates have discovered that lining up outside support is necessary but not sufficient to achieve true, lasting change inside transportation agencies. This is not a problem limited to complete streets policies; public policy scholars of all stripes have recognized that the weak link in a policy initiative is frequently implementation, with a seamless march from policy directive to practice being the exception rather than the rule. During the policy adoption process, many people involved will have experienced a profound shift in their view of the purpose of transportation projects; working together to write and pass the policy, they have built new relationships with one another while building a new, multimodal vision. They have set a new agenda and given the transportation agency a new problem to solve. The trouble is, this transformation has not fully engaged the people who are now responsible for turning the vision into reality, the people who work inside the government transportation agency, or the consultants they hire. These people may not be motivated to change, and as previously discussed, they may be oriented more to building projects than to following policy directives. And even if they are motivated, it is easy to underestimate the extent of the changes being asked of them.

Once the policy is adopted, essentially a whole new effort must begin in order to bring it into daily practice. Too often, it just doesn't happen.

Hawaii's Experience

Hawaii became an early adopter of a state complete streets law pushed by a diverse advocacy coalition that has been a hallmark of the Complete Streets movement. The One Voice for a Livable Island Coalition (now the Hawaii Complete Streets Coalition) included the state AARP chapter, the Hawaii Bicycle League, the Hawaii Public Health Association, and the PATH trails alliance. This coalition launched a successful legislative campaign, earning media coverage by focusing on the issue of pedestrian safety and conducting surveys showing that safer roads were a top priority for older adults in Hawaii. It also brought in outside experts and collaborated closely with state lawmakers on the wording of the legislation. The Hawaii Department of Transportation (HDOT) participated in the discussions with lawmakers on the fashioning of the bill and did not actively oppose it.

Act 054 was signed by Governor Linda Lingle in May 2009 and required HDOT and Hawaii's counties to adopt complete streets policies to go into effect for all projects begun after January 1, 2010. The law created a six-month Complete Streets Task Force to review design standards and propose changes to procedures and design manuals. HDOT was slow in convening the task force, so the first meeting was not held until February 2010. The task force initially worked on recommendations for specific design treatments but then concluded that it was "an overwhelming challenge to reach consensus on preferred design standards" before their final report was due in December. Instead, the task force focused on drafting a statewide policy and "providing guidance of when and where complete streets should be considered and implemented."[1] One advocate termed the final report "very generic." The recommendations in the report were framed more as general suggestions than as specific action items for the state and counties to take.

While the HDOT director who presided over the task force was supportive, in November 2010 a new governor was elected who appointed a new director to run HDOT. Advocates say the new governor and director have little interest in complete streets; HDOT employees say the change of administration, and the need to focus on project delivery, put complete streets on a back burner. HDOT did not adopt the required internal complete streets policy until March 2012. This was days after the chair of the Senate Committee on Transportation and International Affairs, Senator Kalani English, held a briefing on the issue featuring walkability expert Dan Burden. At the briefing, Senator English echoed language used by the task force as he called for "a paradigm shift in our attitudes about road usage and solving our traffic problems." We need to plan communities for all road users and not just for cars."[2]

HDOT's internal policy, which was not released publicly at the time, lists general complete streets principles ranging from safety to energy efficiency. The only implementation step or tool mentioned is a Complete Streets Evaluation Form, which is a yes/no checklist that echoes the general principles stated in the policy and includes a brief space for indicating applicable exceptions. The checklist makes no attempt to integrate the general principles with the way the department currently classifies projects or structures project delivery. In August 2012, HDOT officials said internal implementation meetings were beginning to take place—well more than three years after passage of the law.

It is clear that the leadership in HDOT did not buy into complete streets and that continued project delivery was more important. The political transition didn't help, and Hawaiian proponents of complete streets also attribute the resistance to change to a work culture in which civil servants hold on to their jobs for their entire careers and know they can "outwait the politicians." One observer noted that county public works/transportation directors had the attitude that "this is going to make my job harder, so go away and leave me alone." I suspect that the task force's emphasis on looking at specific design treatments only raised HDOT's hackles further, by stepping directly into the engineers' area of expertise.

Hawaii's experience is not unique; all across the country, complete streets policies end up lying dormant. Sometimes the policy intent gets sidetracked. Oregon's department of transportation, celebrated for its proto-complete streets law dating to 1974, had focused for years only on the law's requirement that 1 percent of funds go to foot trails and bicycle facilities. The state didn't get serious about making its roads safe for everyone until after Portland was sued by advocates in the 1990s for failing to comply with the Bike Bill, and internal champions began to push for institutionalization. Connecticut's more recent complete streets law has the same 1 percent funding requirement, and it seemingly did not spark immediate change. The law directs the state's Bicycle and Pedestrian Advisory Board to oversee implementation, but the board's frustration with the process was palpable from reading their 2011 annual report: "Despite the success that has occurred over the past year, we are discouraged that the requirements of Section 13a-153f (b), after 3 years, have not been fully implemented into the routine practices of would-be 'implementers' of the law."[3] The board, made up of citizen members appointed by the governor and leaders of the state legislature, lists sixteen recommendations, but it is very clear that the board is on the outside, looking in.

Not all complete streets policies are passed by legislative bodies; transportation agencies have also adopted internal directives. These would seem to have a better chance of resulting in changed practices, and many have; as discussed later in this book, New Jersey and California have both made strides with internal policies. But they can also lead nowhere, as in the case of the Virginia policy, adopted in 2004.

How Policies Help with Implementation

The first question to ask about a lack of action is whether the policy itself has not given enough direction or created enough accountability to result in real change. The National Complete Streets Coalition recommends ten elements of an "'ideal'" complete streets policy; all are intended to aid in institutionalization.[4] The Coalition publishes a ranking of written policy content; for example, New Jersey's internal policy is one of the highest scoring, getting the maximum 16 points for addressing implementation planning, and a total score of 85 out of 100. In contrast, Virginia's policy received 4 implementation points, and a total score of 51.[5]

Two of the scored policy elements are directed specifically at creating accountability in the implementation process, by naming implementation next steps and establishing new performance measures. Implementation steps may include naming a responsible agency or person; creating an advisory committee; or requiring a formal implementation plan and annual progress reports. The measures of success can be quantitative or qualitative. For example, Indianapolis requires quantitative measures ranging from crash rates to percentage of transit stops made accessible with sidewalks and curb ramps. In New Hope, Minnesota, the policy suggests qualitative measures, such as tracking the compliments and complaints received from residents.[6]

It is also important that the core policy statement sets a very clear intent that can help guide future action. For example, it can state, as Bozeman, Montana's policy does: "The City of Bozeman will plan for, design, construct, operate, and maintain appropriate facilities for pedestrians, bi-cyclists, transit vehicles and riders, children, the elderly, and people with disabilities in all new construction and retrofit or reconstruction projects subject to the exceptions contained herein." Such a clear statement can be returned to again and again by the people working inside the agency, setting a clear direction as decisions are made about new systems and specific projects.

Policy writers also need to avoid sliding from setting a clear direction into spelling everything out. The seemingly logical urge is to write or up-date the policy so it will create a legally binding standard and "force" the agency to change. Public health lawyers who cut their teeth in the tobac-co wars have written model legislative policies that prescribe the addition of "Complete Streets Infrastructure" to roadway projects, listing the spe-cific items to be added. But changing street design is much more complex than banning smoking. And taking legal action when a road design does not meet expectations is difficult, expensive, relatively rare, and some-times prohibited.[7] Directing an agency to take up the practice of building complete streets means they will be making changes that get at the heart of the professional training, attitudes, and orientation of transportation practitioners. Elected officials can't legislate that transformation, and they shouldn't tread into the territory of prescriptive street design. The respon-sibility of the elected officials is to redefine the problem and then direct the transportation professionals to use their expertise to solve it.

Getting Beyond the Limits of a Written Policy

As the focus shifts from the political realm to agency practice, the policy document itself can only do so much to assist with implementation. The vision statement in the policy may even get in the way. Complete streets vision statements typically list every possible benefit of getting more peo-ple to walk, bike, and take transit, from economic growth to placemaking to health. The potential for such outcomes may have played a big role in initial policy adoption. This exciting vision helped bring on a broad range of constituents and gave them an outlet for years of frustration with the limitations of the transportation industry. However, the emphasis may be lost on agency practitioners, who see those goals as extraneous or even irrelevant to their daily work. Their imperative is to provide transportation infrastructure that speeds automobile travel.

A recent survey of transportation planners and engineers in cities in Oklahoma and Texas illustrates this disconnect. It found that more than 80 percent of these professionals reported that one of the biggest barriers to complete streets policies is the public perception that "other modes are irrelevant/costly/ineffective"; more than 70 percent reported that their colleagues feel that non-automobile modes don't have value.[8] These perceptions are showstoppers. Complete streets proponents add to the skepticism if they frame the issue as one of creating a more sustainable, healthy, livable community by convincing people to start to walk, bicycle, or take the bus. When the agency employees hear about such seemingly unrealistic goals, they may just roll their eyes and get back to work at hand.

The transportation professionals are more likely to be motivated if the problem is framed as one they already care about: the safety of current users of the roadways. In every community, people are already walking, riding bicycles, and catching buses on unsafe streets. Many are those without a choice. About 12 percent of traffic deaths are people on foot and bicycle, and a disproportionate portion of them are older people. The streets are not all that safe for people in cars: crashes kill around 30,000 Americans every year, and traffic crashes are the leading cause of accidental death among children from five to nineteen years old.[9]

The Hawaii DOT policy lists ten principles that "serve as a framework" for implementing complete streets. The first on the list is safety, but the rest range from flexible design to user comfort to energy efficiency to health to green infrastructure. They are not prioritized. While the advocacy campaign for passage of the state law focused on pedestrian safety, a look at the meeting materials used by the Complete Streets Task Force reveals that very little work was done during the meetings to more clearly establish this safety problem, or to motivate the practitioners to begin solving it. Liz Fischer of FHWA's division office in Hawaii, who served on the task force, suggested that a more effective approach would have been to "talk about safety—not community design. The engineers will say, okay, we understand safety; that comes closer to home than 'let's make it beautiful for people.' They can understand it more from a safety perspective than from these other things." Safety is not only the most urgent goal of complete streets; it is one of the few goals that all transportation professionals will agree is a primary part of their job. The complete streets approach is simple and clear enough that practitioners can begin to see the possibility that this is a problem within their capacity to solve.

Safety Is Subversive

Safety is a more subversive issue than you might think. To many traditionally trained engineers, safety is a clear zone along the roadway (without trees) that allows cars to drift off the road and then safely return to their lane; it is guardrails and smooth curves and wide lanes that forgive the humans who err while operating a multi-ton vehicle. But new research shows that while this may be the way to achieve safety on limited-access highways, it doesn't work at all well in urban and suburban areas. Eric Dumbaugh, an associate professor of planning at Florida Atlantic University, has written a series of fascinating papers on this topic. He contends that the safety benefits that "forgiving" freeways deliver are derived not so much from their forgiving design as from their elimination of conflict points—points at which two vehicles can run into each other. Applying the same forgiving techniques to arterial roads with many conflict points—intersections, driveways, pedestrian crossings, and the like—encourages higher speeds and results in more serious automobile crashes. These multilane roadways, lined with strip shopping centers and turnoffs for subdivisions and office parks, are also where most pedestrians die.[10]

A variety of intriguing research now shows that in the urban areas, where most Americans live and travel, safety will improve with a different approach. Per capita crashes are fewer and/or less severe in developed areas with traffic calming measures, grid street networks, multimodal accommodation, and narrower roadways with trees or other "obstacles."[11] The reasons for this safer environment are that, per capita, less driving is taking place, which is associated with fewer crashes; people are driving at lower speeds, which results in fewer and less severe crashes; and less forgiving designs are providing drivers with more appropriate information on safe speeds than do speed limit signs.[12] Other research has found that where more people are out on foot and bicycle, they are less likely to be hit by cars; drivers literally begin to "see" them.[13]

A four- to three-lane road conversion with bike lanes in Bloomington, Minnesota.
(Photos by Steve Elkins.)

Individual techniques used in communities implementing complete streets are also resulting in dramatic safety improvements. Two of these eliminate conflict points. "Road diets," also known as road conversions, typically reduce undivided four-lane roads into two lanes with a center turn lane and add bike lanes and pedestrian medians. Other communities

A crew in Washington, DC, installs a HAWK (high-intensity activated crosswalk) beacon on a busy arterial. These signals are now recommended by the FHWA as a safety countermeasure. (Photo by Barbara McCann.)

call these reconfigurations "rechannelizations" or "right-sizing," but whatever the name, they have clear safety benefits. They reduce speed and eliminate the sight-distance issues that often result in one car broadsiding another, and they result in an overall reduction of crashes of between 19 and 47 percent.[14] A second technique is the modern roundabout, which slashes the number of potential conflict points at an intersection and eliminates the most dangerous, including head-on collisions. The FHWA named roundabouts and road diets among nine new proven safety countermeasures in 2012.[15] Two other new countermeasures named by the FHWA are aimed specifically at pedestrian safety: pedestrian medians or refuge islands, and HAWK signals, a new type of pedestrian-activated signal for use at a midblock crossing.

Embracing the New Safety Paradigm

Despite the accumulation of evidence, it remains a challenge to crack the old safety mind-set inside many agencies. Engineer Jack Broz, who is teaching complete streets to engineers across the state of Minnesota, says traditional engineers insist to him that they *are* focused on safety— they just don't see that their standards are vehicle based and don't protect nonmotorized road users. The key to adopting a new approach is creating an expanded definition of safety to include all road users. Once that transition has been made, the transportation professionals will step up to the task.

In Boston, where the Complete Streets movement embraces sustainability, placemaking, and even "smart" roadways, the broad goals did not stop the city from working closely with their engineers to allay their concerns about safety for drivers as well as other users. A primary issue was allowing narrower standard lane widths. The standard "safe" width for a lane had long been deemed to be twelve feet—in Boston, for the state of Massachusetts, and across the country. While official guidance changed to a flexible ten- to twelve-foot range, the twelve-foot lane has persisted as the most fundamental design parameter out there; in Minnesota, it is even encoded in state law. The traffic engineers in Boston were opposed to relaxing that standard, fearing it would result in less-safe streets. The consultants working with the city created a report showing the existing narrow lanes in Boston and gathering together the latest research on lane widths. A landmark study from 2007 found no safety difference between ten-, eleven-, and twelve-foot lanes in urban areas with a speed limit below forty-five miles per hour.[16] The team also put together examples from other cities using narrower lane widths, showing how their bicycle networks would not be possible if they did not have this flexibility. It became clear that the rigid standard was not necessary and was holding back another policy objective, that of creating a complete bicycle network.

The discussion took place at the same time that the city was battling the state over narrowing automobile lanes in order to fit bicycle lanes on Massachusetts Avenue. The meetings about the lane width issue were tense, and the participants' knowledge that the mayor backed a new approach was critical in making the final determination. In the end, eleven-foot lanes were allowed as standard in Boston's new *Complete Streets Guidebook* (and the state approved the design exception for Massachusetts Avenue).

In Wisconsin, the safety argument convinced the state DOT to stop requiring local jurisdictions to share the cost of installing sidewalks. Bicycle and pedestrian coordinator Jill Mrotek Glenzinski had pointed out that the state paid in full for other safety measures such as medians, so why were sidewalks any different?

Safety is a compelling motivator for building complete streets, but note that when the discussion takes place in the context of a specific crash, it will likely veer off into a discussion of the behavior of the victim. Our culture has a strongly established habit of blaming the pedestrian (or bicycle rider) in a crash; just read a few newspaper stories to see the bias. Many people will assume that anyone hit by a car was someplace he or she shouldn't have been (or at best was wearing dark clothing). It usually takes extra effort to help policy makers, journalists, police, and transportation agency officials see that road design may have played a direct role in a crash. In Jackson, Mississippi, Dr. Scott Crawford, a longtime advocate of complete streets, made this point following the deaths of his friends Donna Williams and Powell Calhoun. They were hit in the street on a frontage road; Donna used a wheelchair, and the sidewalk didn't have curb ramps. In an op-ed published in the *Jackson Clarion-Ledger*, Crawford wrote: "Many may wonder: 'Why were they in the street with a wheelchair?' The answer is simple. Our society hasn't yet decided to build and maintain roadways that are safe for ALL its users, including vulnerable ones like bicyclists and pedestrians, and especially those with disabilities."[17] Note that Crawford hones in on the values inherent in transportation decision making even as he points to the deficiency of the roadway.

Bill Deatherage, of the Kentucky Council of the Blind, walking along
Brownsboro Road before and after sidewalk installation.
(Photos courtesy Anne M. McMahon, Louisville, KY.)

Dirk Gowin, a transportation planning administrator for the Louis-ville Metro Department of Public Works and Assets, says the experience of working through a controversial road diet affirmed his belief that safe-ty is at the core of complete streets success. He watched as people lined up for and against a project on Brownsboro Road (US 42), a four-lane commuter route butting up against a cliff on one side. The project was to replace one travel lane with a sidewalk so residents of the adjacent Clif-ton and Clifton Heights neighborhoods could walk to stores, restaurants, apartments, and the Kentucky School for the Blind. Businesses and com-muters who were worried about traffic congestion organized to oppose the project and launched a website (save42.org). In response, Mayor Greg Fischer delayed the project and opened a new public comment period.

Soon, local bicycle and pedestrian advocates, neighborhood residents, and the Greater Louisville Council of the Blind launched their own cam-paign and created their own website (safe42.org). Gowin zeroed in on the safety message. He did an analysis of all the crashes on the corridor using the FHWA data on proven safety countermeasures. He found that if the changes had been in place at the time, they could have prevented up to 60 percent of the recent crashes in the corridor—including pedestrian deaths. He documented that the road diet would delay drivers by an aver-age of just thirteen seconds. In the end, the mayor, in partnership with a supportive local council member, issued a definitive order to proceed.[18] Gowin plans to keep close track of the safety record on the segment and use it to push for additional road conversions—and he's going to stop using the term *road diet* because, he says, "people don't like to diet."

Once the commitment to accommodate all users is clear, a whole cascade of changes begins to take place. Agencies can make some progress by simply completing sidewalk networks. But they can't fully address nonmotorized safety without also addressing speed, and they can't make more room on the roadway for other users without confronting automobile Level of Service standards. Pretty soon, many agencies find themselves changing fundamental agency practices. This is the topic of the next chapter.

The painting of a green bicycle lane in Washington, DC, came only after the District Department of Transportation (DDOT) made changes to its internal systems and decision-making processes to prioritize safety for all users. (Photo courtesy DDOT–Adolfo Nino.)

CHAPTER FOUR

Process over Projects: Changing How Decisions Are Made

O NCE A POLICY IS IN PLACE, citizens who worked for it may look for complete streets success on the street: Have new bike lanes been installed? Is there a new safe crossing for transit users? They may be caught up in the same common misconception that trips up practitioners—the view that a complete streets approach is "additive," that the main task is to simply add sidewalks, add bike lanes, or add curb ramps and crosswalks. This view is often at the root of concerns about the expense of "adding complete streets components," an issue that is discussed further in chapter 7.

This view can also keep the discussion about change at the project level. In some cases, advocacy groups, and sometimes advisory boards, set themselves up as project watchdogs, challenging design decisions and fighting to wrest some space from automobiles. But a focus on individual projects can chew up a tremendous amount of time and effort—as advocates quickly get caught in what San Diego advocates call an "entrenched policy web [that] favors vehicle movement."[1] While this web of internal policies, rules, standards, and guidelines can be overcome for a single project, it will keep catching future multimodal projects, forcing advocates to struggle toward a more inclusive outcome again and again. Complete streets policies are intended to end this project-by-project approach to change, and they do so by focusing not on projects but on changing the internal guidelines, policies, processes and systems that have been set up to provide for a single mode.

Changing these systems is the way to ensure that policy decisions are brought into daily practice. The use of a "web" metaphor by the San Diego advocates indicates just how sticky the old practices can be—and how thoroughly they can entangle a simple project that was intended to make the street safer. Untangling this web within a department's practices is the first task of complete streets policy implementation. This untangling is achieved by addressing four aspects of an agency's work: its day-to-day decision-making process, the design guidance it uses, how it communicates its mission internally and externally, and, finally, the way it measures success.

Charlotte, North Carolina, a midsized but rapidly growing city in the South, has aligned its entire department of transportation (CDOT) and city to light rail and complete streets, after decades of suburban, automobile-oriented development in which not a single sidewalk was built. Under director Danny Pleasant, CDOT recently produced a brochure entitled, "We Can't Keep Widening Our Roads, so We Have to Broaden Our Thinking." Such broadened thinking is the key to the transformative power of the Complete Streets movement. Places with successful complete streets policies have reexamined their day-to-day procedures and included more people in making decisions. They have educated everyone—citizens, leaders, and practitioners alike—in how to achieve a balance for the mix of users on a particular street. They have broadened the scope of their design manuals, and they are expanding the measures they use to define success. These themes show up in complete streets transitions whether they are taking place in state DOTs or in small towns, as illustrated through the many examples that follow.[2]

Change the Way Projects Are Developed

The disconnected sidewalks, marooned bus stops, curb ramps to nowhere, and other gaps in transportation infrastructure are usually a reflection of gaps in the processes used for planning, design, and construction. In many jurisdictions, no one has thought about how to balance the needs of more than one mode, or how to get the details right on small-scale nonmotorized infrastructure, or how to coordinate transportation planning with the surrounding neighborhood. Another gap is human. The people navigating that landscape by foot or wheelchair were likely not in the room when the decisions were made.

The first way to start filling in these gaps is to be more inclusive: expand the number and type of people involved in making decisions. The next challenge is understanding the shortcomings of the current project development process and creating an implementation plan that will address them. This usually leads to actions that end biases that favor one mode and one type of user and that create entirely new systems to help make decisions.

Be Inclusive

The first and most revolutionary change brought about by most complete streets policies is a meeting. People who work for the planning, public works, and parks and recreation departments usually attend. Representatives from the health department, the development authority, and the water and sewer authority take a seat. Sometimes the city manager's or

Planners and engineers from seven Chicago-area towns plan their transition to a complete streets approach. (Photo courtesy Michael Dannemiller.)

mayor's office sends a representative. In some communities, this meeting includes community groups as well, perhaps from the disability commission, the bicycle advocacy group, or a residents' association. The meeting may begin with a review of the goals of the new policy; usually, the most fundamental is improving safety for all users, but in some communities the most-talked-about goal may be increasing physical activity and health, providing a base for economic growth, or meeting sustainability targets. But this meeting, and those that follow, isn't about lofty goals; it is about what needs to change in the way that people do their jobs.

That's a touchy subject. Lines of responsibility are often clearly drawn. Everyone respects the right of department directors to run their own show. Departments, divisions, and even individual offices control well-defined turf, and they sometimes do not want to relinquish control. One bicycle-pedestrian coordinator told me the departments in his small city operate as "fiefdoms," with each department director working independently on a narrow agenda. If one department, or even one individual in a position of power, doesn't buy into the vision, it can block progress. And in transportation, the turf is viewed in highly technical terms; typically, everyone defers to the expertise of the engineers. One consultant working on complete streets guidelines for a large city called this a "technical shield" that engineers have used to protect themselves from questions as they make decisions on everything from lane width to signal timing.

But once discussions start to take place in an open room, it becomes clear that traditional practices are standing in the way of the new policy objectives—and people can start challenging those traditions. Ryan Snyder, a California transportation consultant and a Complete Streets workshop instructor, says he tries to make these choices clear when he speaks at a meeting that brings together different constituents in a city. If everyone in the room "gets a vote," different decisions start to get made. "Traffic engineers are legitimate stakeholders at the table, but so is the planning department, so is the city manager's office, so are architects and planners, and landscape architects, and of course people from outside [the agency]: the merchants, homeowners, and residents," says Snyder. "Other people should have some say about what happens with their public space."

A committee charged with implementing a policy becomes a driver of change precisely because it provides a forum for different departments to work out problems—if it has the right people in the room. For example, Deerfield Beach, a town in Broward County, Florida, established an internal committee made up of Planning, Engineering, Landscaping, Fire and Rescue, and the City Manager's Office. Many places have established formal advisory boards made up mainly of citizens; they need to work in concert with a staff committee or have strong staff participation and leadership support to be successful in penetrating the agency bureaucracy. Committees can derive energy and focus from zeroing in on a single document or plan. However, communities with time-limited committees or ad hoc groups convened to write a policy or guide find that once the meetings stop, collaboration wanes and past practices may reassert themselves. Ongoing, officially sanctioned committee structures are the most successful route for change.

Project-level teams are another forum for continuing collaboration that can bring together every imaginable agency to weigh in at the beginning of a new project. This has been a hallmark of Seattle's approach to complete streets. The inclusive foundation of Seattle's work goes back to the voters—who approved the nine-year, $365 million "Bridging the Gap" levy in 2006, with an explicit focus on building infrastructure to serve pedestrians, bicyclists, and public transportation. With that backing, the city has not been shy to propose cutting-edge projects, such as road conversions, miniature bus plazas, and colored and buffered bike lanes. The changes are all open to community feedback, and most projects get their own web page, with maps, photos, specific timelines, project contacts, and an opportunity to sign up for e-mail alerts.

An inclusive process also requires maintaining communication as individual projects move forward. Many traditional agencies have rigid stovepipes between planning, engineering, construction, and maintenance: projects are handed off from one to another without much communication. Washington, DC, has tried to break down those divisions in part by ensuring that design drawings made by engineers come back to planning and other concerned agencies as certain points in the process—for example, when they are at 30, 60, or 90 percent completion. At this point, they can be run through the policy sieve and adjusted accordingly—or at least the process can spark a conversation about how to make adjustments.

Duluth, Minnesota, is implementing its complete streets resolution

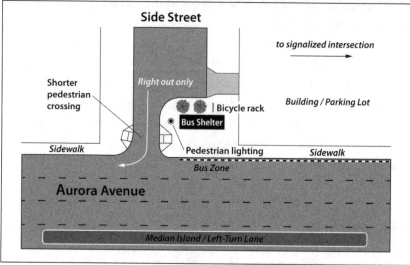

Seattle's bus plazas create more space for bus patrons while
controlling automobile access to neighborhood streets.
(Photo by Barbara McCann; graphic courtesy SDOT.)

primarily through an internal, multidisciplinary complete streets work-
group meeting every month that encourages cross-departmental discussion of each project through the lens of complete streets. The discussions
within this group have greatly influenced the transportation planning
process.

Many agencies are also becoming more sophisticated in making residents part of the decision-making process, and this can itself be a learning

experience. For planners and engineers in Seattle, the realization that they needed to take a different approach came when they gave each neighborhood a small transportation fund of $8,000. Peter Lagerwey, a former Seattle city planner and Complete Streets workshop instructor, was enthusiastic as he told me the story. "Of all of those neighborhoods, *every single one* chose bicycle and pedestrian improvements," said Lagerwey. "Not one chose Level of Service improvements or congestion relief—yet these were the purported goals of our entire transportation program! That is when the light bulb started to go on for some of the staff."

Nashville, Tennessee, engages the public in its decisions via neighborhood-level plans created in close collaboration with residents. The planning process now includes a discussion of complete streets and an emphasis on asking community members to prioritize the projects they want finished to make it safer to walk, bicycle, and take transit. Nashville is also breaking down walls between agencies—when the public works department asked the Metropolitan Transit Agency for its input on the new citywide sidewalk plan, the director of planning at the agency, James McAteer, reached out to bus drivers to find out where on their routes the riders were stepping off into the mud.

In Baldwin Park, California, a majority Latino community in the Los Angeles region, the policy adoption process was directed by two active committees, the Community Task Force and the Partners Task Force of elected officials, practitioners, and representatives from the school district. Members of both task forces took part in a community design charrette to create a plan for converting five major city corridors into more complete streets. This set a good base for participation in the Complete Streets Advisory Council, which now oversees policy implementation and includes members of the very active Baldwin Park Residents Advisory Council, a local health group, the school district, and representatives from the city's public works, planning, policy, and parks and recreation departments. The committee meets quarterly to review and provide recommendations on all upcoming street projects and submits a quarterly report to the city council evaluating progress. The city has also sought input from the Baldwin Park Residents Advisory Council as it has worked to adopt a new design manual based on the *Model Design Manual for Living Streets*, produced by Los Angeles County.[3]

Public health entities have been essential in getting residents engaged and active. In Baldwin Park, the community has been motivated by a health crisis: 39 percent of its children are overweight. The effort was assisted by the long-term support of a grant from the health care consortium Kaiser Permanente. In the Upper Peninsula of Michigan, support from a public health grant allowed the Sault Ste. Marie Tribe of Chippewa to become engaged in transportation planning, working for sidewalks and transit access for youth and older adults who live in the region's small cities. Boston used a federal public health grant program to organize neighborhood walking audits that helped educate residents and cement the support of the mayor as they started their complete streets work.

Understand the Process

At Complete Streets Policy Implementation Workshops offered to jurisdictions by the Coalition, often the first revelation of the day is the discovery that no one in attendance has a clear picture of all the steps involved in choosing, planning, and building transportation projects. But understanding the current process is essential because, in most cases, the project development system dictates how decisions are made. At the workshops, the barriers to a complete streets approach sometimes become obvious, as people from different departments learn about what their counterparts do and then, together, discuss everything that stands in their way. Another way agencies commonly discover these barriers is by launching a multimodal pilot project, but this approach is useful only if a commitment exists to using the experience to change the underlying system. Otherwise, the rules may simply be waived without examination for this one special project.

Advocates who work outside the system also find that understanding it is critical. Ethan Fawley, of the environmental advocacy group Fresh Energy, heads up the Minnesota Complete Streets Coalition, where he's learning about the complexity of the transportation project development process both through the committee's systemic work and through his membership on the Complete Streets External Advisory Committee working with Minnesota's Department of Transportation (MNDOT). "Every so often we peel apart a new rich vein of information," he said as he recounted his discovery that MNDOT had separate sets of engineers, for new construction and for maintenance projects, who work in very different ways. The maintenance engineers focused on putting contracts out to bid and did not do much design work. The advocates figured out that the engineers needed more information for a bike lane being installed as part of a maintenance project. Says Fawley: "They had no idea of the complexity of this road profile; the only measurements they had were done in the 1980s. This turned out to be the most design work these engineers had ever done!" The advocates ended up giving them measurements taken with Google Earth. Advocates and insiders who take the time to understand the roles and responsibilities of the sometimes hundreds of employees in a large agency can then get past the common resentment that so-and-so, or such-and-such a department, "just doesn't get it." Such a personalization of barriers leaves little room for working together to find a solution.

Understanding can come about when people from different agencies, departments, and interest groups meet as part of a committee or an advisory board charged with implementing the policy. In Kauai, Hawaii, the Built Environment Task Force of the public health initiative Get Fit Kauai was directed to oversee complete streets policy implementation for Kauai County, made up of Hawaii's westernmost islands. The task force includes representatives from several county departments, including planning, parks and recreation, health, public works, engineering, and housing, as well as several elected officials. Some members of the task force were unsure if the county's resolution, which lacked teeth, would provide enough impetus to really change practice, and they knew they would need to work hard for implementation. Bev Brody, the facilitator of Get Fit Kauai, is a public health educator, not a transportation professional. So she sought outside help, sponsoring a Complete Streets Implementation Workshop for the practitioners in the county while also seeking out other nationally known experts to provide more detailed advice.

The Built Environment Task Force used their monthly meetings to systematically address changes needed to design standards, subdivision regulations, and performance measures to bring them in line with the complete streets intent. Brody attributes strong support from mayor Bernard Carvalho, but she also notes that when two new engineers came on board at the public works department in 2011, "I glommed onto them. I thought, 'I'm not going to let anyone else warp or wreck their thoughts, they are going to be Complete Streets from the start.'" Brody says the mayor, county engineer Larry Dill, and deputy county engineer Lyle Tabata have all been very clear that Complete Streets and Safe Routes to School are top priorities for the county. Over time, as practitioners inside the county became more knowledgeable, Brody was able to pull back from her hands-on work.

Kauai's experience shows how the policy itself can help point to success if it designates a person or committee to lead implementation—and in Kauai County's case, the policy also created accountability by requiring a report back to the mayor and city council in eighteen months. In some places without a clear lead or plan, departments with different viewpoints have no motivation to work with one another nor any avenue to negotiate their way to new procedures. Each department may take the small steps they can manage on their own, but otherwise they may end up in a stalemate.

Plan for Implementation

Complete streets policy presents such a straightforward goal—safely accommodating all users—that agency officials sometimes assume that they face a design challenge that they can solve in a straightforward way, perhaps by simply writing and distributing a single checklist to ensure planners and designers are aware of the needs of all modes. But such an approach is unable to address that "web" of internal policies and rules that advocates discovered in San Diego. A conscious implementation planning process can help identify all the systems, routines, silos, and assumptions that, together, have created the current transportation project delivery system.

Creating an implementation plan can keep up the momentum begun with policy adoption, and it can help keep partners who were active in policy adoption engaged as the focus shifts to implementation. An implementation plan provides the opportunity to assess current practices, to assign responsibility for making specific changes, and to create estimated timelines for accomplishing those tasks. Doing so creates a tool that the leaders of a complete streets conversion can use to communicate clearly with different departments, outside agencies, community leaders, and advocates.

Minnesota DOT began creating its implementation plan even before the new state law passed in 2010. The plan is divided into nine sections and is set up in a chart format that assigns responsibility and deadlines for each step. The plan covers project development and also addresses planning, funding, communications, and performance measures.[4]

Saint Paul is one of the few cities nationwide that has adopted a formal complete streets implementation plan. The Saint Paul Planning and Economic Development and Public Works Department, working with other city departments as appropriate, created a three-step implementation process, funded in part by a grant from the US Department of Transportation. The process includes three elements: (1) an assessment of the street design process, transportation infrastructure, and network gaps; (2) the writing of a street design manual that will include local and state standards, best practices, and an evaluation of how well street users are served by different design elements; and (3) the design of pilot projects using the new design manual to test and revise the manual as needed.[5]

End the Tilt

At some point in that first meeting after a policy is passed, people will start talking about the potential to put in bike lanes or to reconfigure an intersection. Someone who works for the agency is bound to say, "We can't do that." A key to changing processes is to ask, "Why not?" Dig deeper to discover and change what is tilting the process so that it is difficult to achieve a multimodal balance.

I learned this lesson when researching how regional governments use a particular federal funding program to support bicycling and walking. At the time, about 45 percent of bicycle/pedestrian projects in the Sacramento, California, region were supported by the Congestion Mitigation and Air Quality (CMAQ) program. The Sacramento planner working with the program was enthusiastic, telling me that CMAQ "almost earmarks money for bike/pedestrian" projects, recognizing that they are beneficial to air quality, inexpensive, and easy to implement. In contrast, in the Baltimore MPO, zero CMAQ dollars were used for bicycle/pedestrian projects. In Baltimore, the planner I spoke with said that since it is difficult to show air quality impacts with such projects, they are not competitive for CMAQ funding.

How could both planners be right in their assessment of the potential uses for this program? The answer: each state sets its own rules for spending CMAQ money. California had made a point to write rules that help regions quantify the difficult-to-calculate benefits of nonmotorized projects and to give favorable weight to their much lower cost—and the state provided local control over the program.[6] Maryland's rules used more traditional measures, and regions competed for CMAQ funding at the state level; small localized projects couldn't compete with big projects intended to reduce diesel emissions or improve traffic flow.[7] While the regional planners in both places talked as if the opportunities or limitations of the CMAQ program were set in stone, in fact they were written on paper by agencies—and the bias that the agencies had "baked in" to their program rules had a dramatic impact on the programs' ultimate outcomes.

Jurisdictions large and small can easily discover the programmatic, design, and habitual biases that tilt decisions toward one mode—and then work to change them. Some communities are doing this systematically, by reviewing all documents that might affect transportation—for example, the Seattle complete streets ordinance called for a review of "the Department's Transportation Strategic Plan; Seattle Transit Plan; Pedestrian and Bicycle Master Plans; Intelligent Transportation System Strategic Plan; and other SDOT plans, manuals, rules, regulations and programs as appropriate."[8] A document review should go beyond transportation plans; many communities are revising their zoning codes and subdivision regulations, and more. (For more information about changing the rules that govern roads built by private developers, and those governing maintenance projects, see chapter 5.)

Most commonly, bicycle, pedestrian, and public transportation facilities and considerations for users of different abilities have simply been left out of consideration in the transportation planning process. They can be added in, but the most basic piece of pedestrian infrastructure—the sidewalk—remains at a distinct disadvantage because of rules that commonly separate its funding and maintenance from the rest of the roadway. The practice reaches back to English common law and has often meant that states require local governments to help pay for sidewalks, and that local governments put the cost on property owners.[9] Missoula, Montana, was typical: it had always required residents pay for installation of sidewalks.

The city's complete streets policy prompted the city council to create a subcommittee to grapple with the issue. After months of wrangling over many proposals, the city will now pay the first $1,000 of the installation, will split expenses up to $7,000 with the homeowner, and will cover the rest, up to $15,000. Councilman Jason Wiener told the local newspaper, the *Missoulian*: "It was a heavily deliberative process, but you know, I'm pretty proud of the result. We've done our best to respond to a consistent criticism of the system that we've been using, and hopefully, people will judge this one to be more fair."[10] A few cities have simply taken on all responsibility for building sidewalks. A few northern cities now clear sidewalks of snow on designated routes because a reluctance to shovel has led to resistance to sidewalk installation.

As discussed in chapter 1, one of the most common practices that tilts the transportation system toward providing for automobiles is the use of automobile Level of Service ratings as a primary method of choosing and designing transportation projects. Some places are making relatively small adjustments to the system, such as reconfiguring LOS to measure and set standards for off-peak travel, instead of focusing only on rush hour; relaxing LOS standards and accepting higher levels of congestion at certain intersections or in certain areas; or exempting projects from having to meet LOS standards. Some places are using different types of LOS that give a service ranking for nonmotorized users; these new LOS standards are usually qualitative evaluations of the bicycle, pedestrian, and transit environment and are often used alongside of traditional volume-based automobile LOS. But some experts reject these new Level of Service models and suggest ditching the whole system. San Francisco is experimenting with a new citywide system of estimated auto trips generated to measure the impact developments will have on traffic.[11] Some places, notably New York City, now use a calculation of "person delay" rather than vehicle delay, which takes into account the dozens of people who may be in a single vehicle—such as a city bus.[12]

Maintenance and operations projects almost by definition are about maintaining the status quo—and that status quo is too often an incomplete street. Commonly, the only criterion for selecting and designing these projects is pavement condition and keeping costs low; there is no time or money devoted to redirecting these projects to help retrofit a more multimodal design. But these projects, usually carried out by the public works department, can be the best opportunity to quickly create change within communities. In some places, they will be the primary opportunity for change because each year they affect much more of the road network than new capital improvement projects. Their incremental nature is also an important asset in the transition to a complete streets approach. Chapter 5 explores this opportunity in more detail.

In addition to being tilted toward automobiles, transportation planning and design have been tilted toward the driver and the able-bodied—even in communities with significant numbers of children, older people, and households without cars. A well-known national bias was recently corrected when the *Manual of Uniform Traffic Control Devices* changed its guidelines for estimating how fast pedestrians can walk across the street by lowering the standard—the old standard had been based on briskly moving college students.

Create New Systems

The process of ending a systemic bias toward cars usually means developing new systems that are more inclusive. Here, too, communities respond with a continuum of change. Sometimes the new systems are narrowly defined and laid over current processes. Other jurisdictions have decided that the most effective thing to do may be to start from scratch—to invent new systems that do a better job of taking into account the needs of all users.

CHECKLISTS: A common first technique used by many jurisdictions is the creation of checklists that remind or require planners and engineers to consider the needs of all users as they go about their work, and particularly as they scope and propose projects. A checklist approach can help provide appropriate solutions based on transportation and land use needs and can also help collect and share information. Checklists can ensure that at each stage of a project, from scoping to construction, the needs of all users are accounted for and appropriately accommodated.

The regional planning agency in Columbus, Ohio, the Mid-Ohio Regional Planning Commission, established a comprehensive questionnaire that walks local jurisdictions through all the factors they should consider in planning a road system for all users. While called a checklist, it also asks project sponsors to fill in data about the existing roadway, the goals for improving it, and the types and numbers of people and vehicles traveling. The checklist covers everything from scoping to public input and has functioned as a teaching tool for the region. As is common with checklists, it asks for an explanation when safe facilities for all users are not part of the project.

Hennepin County, Minnesota, has developed a checklist that is now being used on all projects. The checklist covers existing and proposed features of the roadway; intersections; utilities; bicycle and pedestrian facilities; and presence of transit. It also asks about features along the roadway, such as schools, fire stations, and parks. Project managers use the checklist at the beginning of the design process on street reconstruction projects and update it as the project evolves. The county's diversity of roads—350 of which are classified as urban and 223 as rural—demands a context-specific approach. The extensive checklist helps provide this needed measure of flexibility. It continues to evolve, as it is tested with each new project.

While checklists can by themselves be a central feature of basic complete streets policies, increasingly they are being used as guides that summarize or organize complex new systems detailed in new design manuals, such as those being developed in Philadelphia, Dallas, and Chicago, as well as in New Jersey and North Carolina.

EXCEPTIONS: Most complete streets policies spell out specific exceptions to the policy—cases in which streets will be built or (more commonly) rehabilitated without safety features for bicyclists, pedestrians, or transit users. (Federal guidance on bicycle and pedestrian travel suggest exceptions on roads where nonmotorized users are prohibited; where agencies can document a lack of need now and in the future; and in projects in which costs are excessively disproportionate to need.) Usually, a system is needed to determine when and how exceptions to the policy are made. In many cases, the parameters of the exceptions are spelled out in the policy document, but not the process by which they are sought and approved. This process can be explicitly political: while the conflict may begin with a technical problem (such as not enough right-of-way), its resolution usually involves a judgment call. People with power need to make these decisions. Individual exception requests are often hotly debated as agencies start down the road toward complete streets, when anxiety is high among engineers who are worried about having more to do and maintain, and among citizens who want to preserve their car commute or parking. As time goes on, the furor usually subsides, as the process becomes clearer.

Rochester, Minnesota's policy specifies that all street construction, reconstruction, and resurfacing and re-striping projects have to be evaluated for complete streets applicability. The city engineer is tasked with determining appropriateness of a complete streets approach. An internal staff project review by the city engineer, traffic engineer, and director of public works ensures compliance with the policy or, in some cases, approves technical exceptions. But the final decision on an exception is made by the city council. Public involvement meetings, made more common after the policy's adoption, help to inform community members and leaders of proposed road design and safety solutions. If significant opposition is expressed during these meetings, the project is taken to council. A few proposed complete streets treatments were rolled back during the first year of implementation due to citizen opposition. The public works department now makes sure the council has received basic information about all upcoming projects, and recently the process has become routine; the council has not been approving many exceptions.

An exceptions clause is listed as one of the ten basic elements of an effective complete streets policy. But in many communities, an emphasis on an exceptions process has given way to developing greater clarity about how different streets will function.

Starting from Scratch: Many places have found that ending biased decision making, adding new checklists, and creating an exceptions process are not enough to fully integrate all the new information they are putting into the transportation decision-making process. In the past, transportation projects required a consideration of just a few factors: the volume of cars, the amount of congestion, and the documented crash rate. Now they need to account for what types of people are using the road (older adults? children?), how they are traveling (driving? public transportation? walking?), and what type of neighborhood they pass

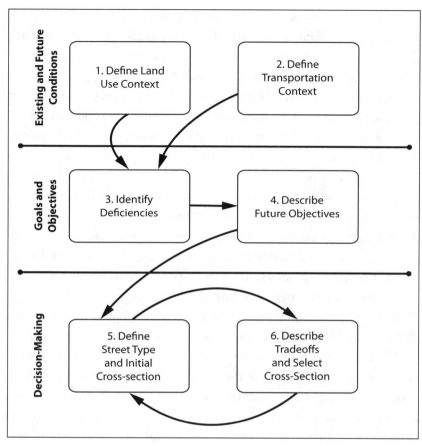

Charlotte's six-step planning process, from the *Urban Street Design Guidelines*.
(Courtesy Charlotte DOT.)

through (industrial? business district? residential?). They also need to involve the public and to be accountable to broader transportation goals.

One solution is to bring all the procedural changes together by creating an entirely new project development process. The most well-known is the six-step process created by the Charlotte Department of Transportation in its *Urban Street Design Guidelines*,[13] also used as a teaching tool in the National Complete Streets Coalition workshops. This six-step process was developed specifically to deal with the complexity and detail that seems necessary to create complete streets. The process starts by evaluating the existing land use and transportation context of the project;

moves on to identify gaps and deficiencies and to define future objectives; and then recommends a street classification and deliberates the trade-offs that might need to be made. Charlotte planners and engineers apply the process to all plans and projects that could affect existing streets or result in new streets, including area plans, streetscape plans, neighborhood improvement plans, development proposal reviews, and preparation of the capital improvement plan. The scope and complexity of any project directly influences the complexity of the corresponding six-step process and the degree of public involvement.

By starting with an evaluation of existing conditions, this process ensures that planners cover all the factors that need to be considered, and this helps prevent a jump straight into a presumed treatment or solution. The middle steps, identifying gaps and objectives, bring clarity and focus to the fifth step, the proposed street cross section. Charlotte is using a new street classification system that provides for a range of travel priorities, from parkways that emphasize automobile throughput, to local streets that are aimed at serving the residents who live along them.

The last step, the discussion of trade-offs, is perhaps the most important, because it recognizes that the rationality of the previous steps won't necessarily lead to a cut-and-dried solution. The process makes room for the inevitable push and pull of balancing the needs of different users.

While Charlotte found working with the North Carolina DOT to be a struggle in the first few years, NCDOT is now also adopting this process in its new Complete Streets Guidelines. Other places are also revamping their fundamental procedures, and some are doing so in the context of creating new design manuals.

Proponents should not miss opportunities to update relevant plans that guide community development and growth, such as the comprehensive plan, transportation and mode-specific plans, and subdivision and zoning ordinances. These documents often provide the backbone for project selection, compile data that provide the justification for the complete streets approach, and outline preliminary ideas about context and needs. Charlotte's new system is embedded in the city's old planning process and was first articulated in the *Transportation Action Plan*, the transportation element of the comprehensive plan.

In Rochester, the complete streets initiative has focused around systematic change to guiding documents. At the same time that it approved its complete streets policy in the spring of 2009, the city council approved an amendment to the land use plan and to the comprehensive plan, both revised to reflect a more multimodal approach. Since then, the city has written new Downtown Design Guidelines and a Downtown Master Plan and Mobility Study. The new Downtown Master Plan establishes goals for reducing single-occupancy vehicle travel and increasing walking, bicycling, transit use, and carpooling. Most recently, the city completed a new Bicycle Master Plan.

Metropolitan Planning Organizations have taken a leading role in creating handbooks or tool kits for their member agencies that provide many avenues for creating new systems. The Sacramento Area Council of Governments produced one of the earliest complete streets tool kits, which has become an impressive online compendium of all things complete streets.[14] The regional planning agencies for New Orleans and Columbus, Ohio, have written handbooks as well. In the Kansas City region, the handbook's contents are tailored to meet the needs of jurisdictions that are "just getting started," "moving forward," and "building upon success."[15] The content in these handbooks and some of the new plans overlaps with the content of the stand-alone design manuals discussed in the next section. While a bit confusing, this is a reflection that a more holistic, network approach is beginning to drive all parts of the transportation project development and construction process.

Change Design Guidelines

One could argue that design manuals are just another element of changing the decision-making process. But they have such an outsized influence in the transportation field that they deserve their own category. It is no wonder that revising local or state manuals to be more supportive of multimodal efforts receives the lion's share of attention when it comes time to implement a complete streets approach.

However, an exclusive focus on revising a manual may keep communities in the technical trap. A focus on design specifics to the exclusion of the bigger vision and process can slow down the change process and make it seem insurmountable. Design manual rewrites typically take two to three years to complete. In Hawaii, the Complete Streets Task Force that was appointed following passage of the complete streets law became overwhelmed by design specifics. The task force finally set them aside, but this left little time during their six-month tenure to find ways to really begin to change the approach of the department. Progress ground to a halt for two years. Focusing on design can also leave highway engineers firmly in the driver's seat, and if they have a traditional approach, they can easily knock down proposals for change. This is a dynamic that stalled many reform efforts begun before the Complete Streets movement helped separate the goal of safety for all users from the particulars of design. Nailing down exact design specifications may be less important than becoming clearer about how design decisions will be made.

Agencies spend a lot of time and money on design manual rewrites. Even then they may still not be enough to change the day-to-day workings of an agency. Louisville introduced one of the first complete streets design manuals in 2007, to much fanfare. But the manual has not been well used; planner Dirk Gowin says his department found that the manual's specific cross sections were too prescriptive. And he notes that since it was completed in 2007, the state of the practice has advanced considerably, which is not reflected in the manual. He would like to see a manual that gives him more decision-making tools, rather than prescriptive cross sections.

Many new national resources are available that may help some jurisdictions shortcut the process of writing their own manual. The *Model Design Manual for Living Streets* invites this use; it is available in several formats to allow cutting and pasting.[16] The Institute of Transportation Engineers' *Designing Walkable Urban Thoroughfares* begins to bring land use into the equation, and the National Association of City Transportation Officials, a group representing large cities, is producing a series of guides that push the envelope with innovative treatments.[17] And some proponents firmly believe that the current edition of the AASHTO Green Book allows all sorts of designs that lead to complete streets—if it is used correctly.[18]

New Jersey, California, and Minnesota are all making relatively small, targeted changes to their existing highway design manuals. In New Jersey, the bicycle/pedestrian staff has taken the lead on writing up bicycle and pedestrian components to add to the existing design manual. California has sprinkled changes throughout their *Highway Design Manual* to better accommodate pedestrians, bicyclists, and transit, including space reallocation—e.g., allowing narrower, eleven-foot automobile lanes and extending the curb to create "busbulbs" to make it easier to board buses. The manual also adds a new section on bus rapid transit. Caltrans has also produced a "Complete Intersections" guide and is working on guides for main streets and for system planning.[19] In Minnesota, the rural county engineers who dominate the State Aid Standards committee recently invited two complete streets advocates to attend and speak at their meeting, which was a big change from the past. The head of Minnesota's complete streets effort expects both the "State Aid" and "Trunk Highway" standards to soon allow narrower lanes.

Rather than rewriting manuals, some places have taken a more hands-on approach to design changes by trying out new ideas and keeping those that work. While New York City adopted a new design manual, it doesn't try to answer all the questions. The city has led the way in installing temporary treatments and watching how they work before making them permanent. The town of University Place in Washington prefers to design through community charrettes. Standards are not even allowed in the room during the charrette, where citizens and experts alike are encouraged to use fresh thinking.[20] Many smaller cities, such as Rochester, Minnesota, do not have their own design manuals, preferring to use a variety of national resources.

A number of states and larger cities are approaching design changes by creating new manuals that are presented as supplements to existing guidance or are integrated with other transportation planning documents. The approach and organization of these manuals, handbooks, and guidelines varies widely, but most speak not only to practitioners but also to ordinary citizens by using attractive graphics, photographs, and nontechnical language to convey basic complete streets principles. Agencies can write the manuals as part of an extended process that may also help the agency achieve two other steps to complete streets implementation: working out new procedures and training and educating officials and residents on the complete streets approach. Both the City of Boston and Kauai County, Hawaii, have been writing new manuals slowly, one chapter at a time. In Boston, the writing process has become their education process. Director of policy and planning Vineet Gupta says this has allowed people from different departments to work out conflicts—this was the forum for the difficult discussions over lane width mentioned in chapter 3. "We encouraged the detailed discussion on these issues, because it means in the future it won't just be on a piece of paper, it will be something people have experience with," says Gupta.

The most innovative new manuals go far beyond simple cross sections and have created new ways to tackle the transportation–land use connection. They often create new street typologies. This provides greater nuance than is available through the traditional functional classification system, which divides all roads into three classes exclusively according to their function for automobiles. Many of the new typologies require defining streets in relation to the surrounding land use, sometimes using a model called the Transect, a system created by the new urbanist movement that divides land use into zones ranging from rural to densely urban. Some, such as Nashville's Major and Collector and Street Plan,[21] create two interlocking typology systems, one that focuses on how the street functions for travelers, and the other on how it interacts with surrounding land use. Other systems integrate these features in a single set of typologies.[22]

The best of these manuals do not stop at design particulars. They also help planners and engineers make decisions in a new way—especially with the balancing act now necessary when choosing how to serve competing transportation interests. Charlotte's Urban Street Design Guidelines are notable for the way they put the decision-making process front and center. In the Chicago area, the Active Transportation Alliance produced a model design manual, *Complete Streets, Complete Networks*,[23] with a strong emphasis on process. The manual suggests the creation of new street typologies defined by both the users of the street and the surrounding context. The final chapter details a two-phase process for using the new typologies and supports each with a checklist. The manual is intended for use by many small communities across the Chicagoland area and was funded as part of a bigger Centers for Disease Control and Prevention grant to make policy changes to improve health. The manual recently won an award from the Illinois chapter of the American Planning Association. The City of Chicago has issued its own complete streets design guidance, which helps decision making with a simple and clear directive: put pedestrians first.[24]

The draft *Dallas Complete Streets Design Manual*[25] and chapter 6 of Boston's forthcoming Complete Streets Guidelines both discuss new decision-making systems. Other manuals don't lay out a specific process but include new decision-making tools that help break down complexity and rationalize decisions; the *Philadelphia Complete Streets Design Handbook* revolves around a matrix detailing elements and standards for street types and intersections.[26]

Educate and Train

Early on in thinking about complete streets implementation, the idea of training seemed a pretty obvious category to cover. The National Complete Streets Coalition was asked over and over again for training assistance on design specifics aimed at practitioners. They wanted to know how wide bike lanes should be, what curb radii to use, how to design a pedestrian median. But we soon realized that technical training was only a small part of the learning that needed to take place. Practitioners need to understand the new processes and priorities being put in place. Communication with the public is essential to determine what people want out of their streets and to explain what is happening as roads get new treatments. Elected officials also need ongoing engagement to understand how the general policy goal is being translated into projects on the ground. Practitioners in places that were building projects shifted from asking for design help to asking for public outreach help as citizens questioned and even opposed what they were trying to do. It became clear that the idea of "training" needs to expand beyond design training for practitioners to include procedural training, and also to encompass ongoing education and communication with decision makers and the general public.

Transportation Professionals

Several large state agencies have launched their own complete streets training programs. Massachusetts adopted its revamped *Project Development & Design Guide* in 2006 but found years later that it still hadn't really penetrated all the districts. In 2011, the state created a system of dozens of three- and six-hour training sessions that elaborated on specific points in the manual and what they meant for practitioners working for the state and local agencies across Massachusetts. New Jersey and North Carolina have also conducted formal statewide training programs, and California and Minnesota are working on them.

The sessions aim to do more than provide technical know-how. At training sessions held by the New Jersey DOT, engineers were invited to bring in projects they were working on so others could offer advice. Sheree Davis, the bicycle and pedestrian coordinator for the state, recounts that at one session an attendee brought in a project and the first thing he said was, "This project is exempt under two of the [complete streets policy] exemptions." Davis says other people in the room challenged him and started to discuss what changes might be possible, and soon he started to see the potential as well. Davis says, "In the beginning, people needed permission to do this. We needed to tell them, YOU have permission to be creative here!"

This story shows that while technical training is useful, what is more important is for transportation engineers and planners to understand and embrace the intention behind complete streets as a continuation of their professional development, not a repudiation of it. This will help motivate them to make changes in their procedures, documents, and projects. They need to hear how this approach works in other communities, and how it fits into their professional goals and standards. The best messengers for these sessions are those within the same profession: engineers need to hear directly from other engineers; planners, from other planners.

Dozens of communities have hosted at least one of the National Complete Streets Coalition's Complete Streets Workshops, which are aimed mainly at agency professionals but usually include a component for elected officials and engaged community members.[27] The introductory workshop gives a taste of a complete streets planning process, the policy writing workshop helps a jurisdiction get all the right people in the room to begin to write a policy tailored to their community, and the implementation workshop focuses on how to take the policy into everyday practice. In each case, the workshops are led by two people, one with a planning background and one an engineering professional. The leaders can speak to attendees as peers and help them understand the approach and answer their questions. By day's end of the most successful workshops, the instructors have been all but forgotten as participants focus on the new connections they've made and the inclusive decision-making process they are about to launch.

As previously mentioned, educational opportunities can also be found in the process of writing up new standards and procedures—in Boston, the development of the Complete Streets Guidelines began with eighteen months of presentations and discussion before any decisions were made. Many agencies, particularly smaller cities, have used a more informal, on-the-job approach, with colleagues learning from one another.

Elected Officials and the Public

Work with elected officials and the general public must continue past the adoption of the policy. The support built during the vision-infused policy adoption phase can erode as real projects come up—and face real opposition. Community advocates can be the most effective in providing this ongoing information. Local smart growth groups, the YMCA, AARP, environmental organizations, and bicycling and walking advocates have all brought in outside experts and documented and celebrated early success to support complete streets in their communities. Public health advocates and practitioners have an important role to play in the educational process. Many public health agencies have been sponsors of complete streets workshops, summits, and webinars. They have also sponsored walking audits in which participants conduct a formal assessment of a neighborhood's safety problems, an activity that can be essential in bringing practitioners, decision makers, and ordinary citizens together to discuss and learn about complete streets.

Transportation agency staff can work with these other proponents of complete streets to communicate how the new approach will benefit the community and nearby residents and businesses, and how incomplete streets affect mobility and access to shops, offices, and schools. Many jurisdictions have created their own complete streets web pages. A number have also produced sophisticated short videos to tout the health, economic, and safety benefits of changing street design.[28] Keeping the overarching goals of the policy front and center can help diffuse conflicts that arise when the discussion turns to particular projects. (More discussion on project-level communication appears in chapter 6.)

Measure Success in New Ways

In talking to enthusiastic transportation agency professionals about all the changes they are making to institutionalize complete streets, all the energy suddenly leaves the room when the conversation turns to finding new ways to measure success: "Oh, we haven't gotten to that yet." Very few agencies are tackling this is any systematic way. Performance measures tend to be viewed as a dreaded assignment that no one can find time for, particularly under the strain of budget and staff cutbacks.

Maybe one reason for the lack of enthusiasm is that the primary performance measures traditionally used by the industry are boring, failing, or even frightening. Boring: pavement condition. Of course people don't want potholes, but their repair is not a scintillating subject. Failing: automobile Level of Service. As discussed earlier, LOS defines success as free-flowing traffic, and congestion as failure. Yet, for reasons I won't go into here, traffic congestion almost never shows an improvement—and if it does, it tends to be short-lived or attributed to a negative effect unrelated to agency actions, such as an economic downturn. Frightening: traffic fatalities. Nationwide, traffic safety has improved, as fewer Americans have died on the roadways. But tens of thousands of people still die or are maimed every year, and a positive report just means things are "less bad."

In contrast, academics and advocates get really excited about the potential to show how new transportation investments are having a positive impact. Public health proponents immediately want to know if complete streets policies have performed by getting more people walking and bicycling, and whether that has lowered the average body mass index of the population. Elected officials want to see economic vitality restored to downtown. Environmental advocates believe that complete streets policies should perform in terms of lowering greenhouse gas emissions. All of these outcomes are several steps and potentially years removed from an actual roadway project.

Between these two attitudes is a chasm called data collection. While academics and high-level officials create ambitious but vague goals, agency practitioners have few tools to even begin to connect them to their daily work. The data collected to measure pavement condition, Level of Service, and traffic fatalities are woefully inadequate to answer the bigger questions that start to get asked under the values-driven process sparked by the complete streets approach. There is no question that the transportation industry is in desperate need of more positive ways to talk about its success.

But it doesn't have much to start with. Even the most basic facts are unknown: no inventory exists of "complete" versus "incomplete" streets; even a project list is usually hard to come by. Most jurisdictions have a very limited understanding of the travel mix, because people who walk and bicycle literally don't count—and have never been counted.

The responsibility for strong performance measures really comes back to the political process. The policy adoption process identified values; the community's leadership needs to make sure that it goes on to quantify specifically how the transportation system will support those values. The push for "hard," scientific data can make performance measures more complex than they need to be, according to Jeffrey Tumlin, author of *Sustainable Transportation Planning*. If the goals of the system include residents' feelings of safety and satisfaction, the definition of performance metrics needs to expand to include "soft" data, such as surveys.

All is not lost—a few sophisticated performance metric systems have been devised and are being put into practice, which I will get to in a minute.[29] But given the starting point for most communities, two activities deserve attention as starting points that can build the base for a stronger performance measurement system and that might raise agency enthusiasm for measuring success: counting everyone and everything, and conducting before and after studies.

For many communities, progress in this area begins with simply counting. The most common activity reported by agencies is a recording of the "outputs" of the new policy: the simple counting of new facilities built (or built differently). This shows that the community is making on-the-ground changes, and the annual numbers can show the pace of change over time. Communities can measure not only new facilities but also maintenance activities, such as repairs to curb ramps and repainted bicycle lanes. The regional planning organization can aggregate this data, as, for example, the Fargo-Moorhead Metropolitan Council of Governments does.

The reward can be immediate, as elected officials and the public learn about the scope and extent of the transition to complete streets. It also helps avoid a focus on one or two controversial projects. New Haven, Connecticut, reports that more than thirty roads were improved for all users in the four years following the adoption of the city policy. Every year in its annual report on its "Bridging the Gap" levy, Seattle's Department of Transportation lists dozens of projects that have brought more balance into the transportation system, reporting (here in figures from 2011) such items as miles of bike lanes striped (15), crossing improvements (51), and urban trees planted (822). Each year, the report repeats the nine-year goals of the levy and gives totals so taxpayers can see how they are doing.[30] Talk about transparency.

Measuring ambitious desired outcomes, such as lower greenhouse gas emissions or more physical activity, needs to start with another type of counting: the collection of the basic information of who is traveling and how. Many communities are starting to count the number and/or portion of people walking and bicycling, a seemingly simple measure that was either never taken in the past or recorded only every several years as part of travel diary surveys. Plenty of new tools are coming on line for this task. MNDOT has established a standard methodology for simple manual counts, using the National Bicycle and Pedestrian Documentation Project.[31] The agency is holding workshops to teach it to jurisdictions across the state; Rochester made its first count in the fall of 2012 and hopes to count twice a year. Louisville is using videotape technology to conduct highly accurate twelve-hour counts. The San Diego Association of Governments (SANDAG) has used public health funds to purchase sixty automated counters that use infrared sensors and electromagnetic loops to detect pedestrians and bicycles. Travel surveys are another way to obtain information about trips as well as their purpose and quality. As these data begin to accumulate, jurisdictions can see whether trends develop in non-motorized use overall and along certain corridors. This can be the first indication of any change in the way people are traveling.

A simple step toward performance measurement is at the project level—when "before and after" data collection can show direct and immediate benefits of a transportation investment. This can be especially powerful with road diets or conversions, which typically show a dramatic reduction in speeding, crashes, and crash severity, and sometimes also show an increase in nonmotorized use or even in user satisfaction. SANDAG is now requiring communities receiving special grant funds to collect before data; the agency will go back and record after data itself. In Charlotte, the transportation department is including before counts as part of consulting contracts when planning a project and is considering including after counts as well.

The next step to measuring success can also start with the basics. As previously mentioned, Kauai, Hawaii's Built Environment Task Force launched a very deliberate implementation planning process. Pushed by a member who is a health evaluator, the task force tackled performance measures by assigning each committee member a measure to research: Where would the data come from, and what would be a reasonable measure of success? The measures selected are pedestrian and bicycle crash rates, vehicle miles traveled per capita, percentage of students walking and biking to school, transit usage, mode share for active transportation, miles of bicycle and pedestrian facilities, and miles of street retrofits.

The Promise of Performance Measures

A few communities have unlocked the secret that performance measurement is the key to long-term community support and steady funding. New York City is the best example of this. Even at the level of basic performance reporting, New York City sets a gold standard with its annual Sustainable Streets Index. The index is not a dry report passed around and forgotten at a city council meeting. Large, full-color photographs cover almost every page, overlaid by fascinating, accessible statistics about the transportation system. NYCDOT reports on the basics, including levels of driving, transit use, bicycling, and walking, and on safety. It reports on system quality, using a unique taxi-based GPS system to report traffic congestion levels for every single day of the year. And it provides detailed reports on the major projects conducted in the prior year, with before and after statistics and easy to understand evidence of success; for example, the 2011 edition reported: "New bus and bike lanes on First and Second Avenues in Manhattan improved bus speeds by 15–18%, increased bus ridership by 12% and cycling volumes by 18–177%, and reduced crashes by up to 37%."

Reread that last sentence. These are the type of results that advocates,

35% decrease in injuries to all street users (8th Ave)

58% decrease in injuries to all street users (9th Ave)

Up to 49% increase in retail sales (Locally-based businesses on 9th Ave from 23rd to 31st Sts., compared to 3% borough-wide)

Left turn bays and signal phases

Mixing zones for bicycles and left-turning vehicles

Parking-protected bike lane

Pedestrian safety islands

New York City's Department of Transportation has issued several publications that show how reporting on system performance can be an exciting way to engage the general public. This graphic is from *Measuring the Street: New Metrics for 21st Century Streets.* (Image courtesy NYCDOT.)

practitioners, and elected officials yearn for and constantly request. Results like these have power—yet few agencies seem to understand that a small investment in measuring success is becoming the crucial base for building more support in an era of constrained transportation funding. The performance of complete streets can become a powerful selling point for future projects and funding.

New York has also reached into databases beyond its own department to show how its projects are contributing to economic growth and sustainability—for example, see its publication *Measuring the Street: New Metrics for 21st Century Streets*, which uses real estate and sales tax data to make its case (also see chapter 7 of this book for specifics on its findings). Other agencies are following suit; a New Jersey roundtable on performance measures concluded with attendees choosing the top ten metrics that should be pursued to evaluate the success of the state complete streets policy. Along with more obvious measures of transportation performance, the attendees picked measures such as property values, property occupancy rates, crime rate, business revenue, and health statistics.

Such broader measures of success cannot be the responsibility of the transportation department alone, and they will require collaboration with and leadership from other departments, sectors, and often universities. Many communities making progress in this area started long before they passed a complete streets policy; in California, the San Francisco Bay Area's regional transportation planning agency, the Metropolitan Transportation Commission (MTC), set performance goals in response to a state law passed in 2002. MTC created "stretch" targets, including achieving a 10 percent reduction from today in the percent of income spent on housing and transportation by low-income households.[32]

Performance measures can be an important catalyst to spark change. Boulder, Colorado, resolved in 1996 to hold vehicle miles traveled to 1994 levels. This was to be achieved by reducing single-occupancy trips to 25 percent of total trips by 2025 and increasing the share of trips taken by other modes. The city has kept close track of its progress, and in 2012, it reported that single-occupancy vehicle trips have fallen by about 15 percent since 1991 but that the annual rate of decline needs to double to reach the goal by 2025. Since 1991, bicycling has increased by 75 percent and bus use has soared by 300 percent, while walking has remained at around 18 percent of all trips. The city has succeeded in holding the level of vehicle miles traveled steady.[33] Surely, this wouldn't have happened without the strong goal, and the commitment to meeting it. New measures of success can begin to influence what projects are selected in the first place, which is addressed in chapter 8.[34]

As the move toward multimodal transportation planning matures, more sophisticated and innovative transportation performance measures will no doubt come into play; this section has only touched on the possibilities. But during the transition, agencies can reap immediate benefits from tracking even the simplest of metrics.

Nashville, Tennessee, has made many small improvements, including this bike lane and improved bus stop. (Photo by Gary Layda, City of Nashville.)

Proof in the Projects

Of course, what everyone wants to see in the end are changes on the street. It should be clear by now that the hallmark of a community committed to complete streets is not a single beautiful, innovative boulevard that took years to plan and build. That boulevard may feature a protected bike lane, pedestrian bulb-outs, and transit prioritization features, but the next block over, and the rest of the road network, could be no more than a conduit for fast-moving cars. Supporters should instead look for the many ways, big and small, that the city, county, or state is making all of its roads safer and more inviting.

Projects should reflect both volume and variety every year, as Seattle demonstrates in its "Bridging the Gap" report. Rochester, Minnesota, is tracking road conversions, bike lane striping, and even small steps, such as adjusting signal timing to better accommodate pedestrians, installing more bicycle parking racks, and upgrading wheelchair ramps and school crossings. In Charlotte, the city is systematically retrofitting its streets for all users: as of mid-2012 it had finished or was planning twenty-seven conversions, nineteen intersection redesigns, and twenty-six thoroughfare rebuilds and has instituted more than one hundred sidewalk projects.

A project mix like this is evidence that jurisdictions have been busy working to revamp their decision-making processes, rework their design parameters, and devise new performance measures. In short, they are learning a new way of doing business. No single to-do list exists that will work for every community of every size. The next chapter explores the varied paths to success.

One of many road conversions maintenance crews
installed in Salt Lake City in 2011.
(Photo by Colin Quinn-Hurst, Salt Lake City
Transportation Division.)

CHAPTER FIVE

Looking for Every Opportunity

AS DISCUSSED IN THE LAST CHAPTER, practitioners in every community must address many aspects of their work to fully institutionalize a complete streets approach. But jurisdictions of different sizes and types face different implementation challenges and will focus on different aspects of the conversion.[1] And practitioners guiding new projects launched by private developers will take different actions from those who are managing maintenance of the existing road system. The key is for all practitioners to understand and take advantage of the varied opportunities to make changes that result in safer streets for everyone.

People at state departments of transportation tend to think big—to them, multimodalism primarily means thinking about heavy rail, freight, transit, and ports.[2] And many DOTs focus on rural areas and are more concerned about preventing a collision between a logging truck and a combine than about individual passenger transportation. The Minnesota Department of Transportation's complete streets implementation work plan confronts the question of mission head-on, noting that state highways perform essential services beyond making motor vehicle and freight connections. It notes that highways also provide safe routes to school, serve as community main streets, and provide high-frequency transit routes.[3]

State DOTs are usually huge departments, marked by big bureaucracies, typically with division offices and hundreds of employees spread across the state. It can take some time for complete streets champions to understand what needs to change and how to change it, as is noted in chapter 6 by current and former DOT employees. All of this means that state implementation is likely to be slow and tends to focus first on communication and training; several states have launched formal state-wide training programs.

The scope of responsibility of state DOTs also varies. In at least five states, the state agency owns and operates not only the primary state highways but also secondary roads that serve local communities.[4] At the other end of the scale, a municipal consent statute in Minnesota requires the DOT to get project-level approval from local governments. In every case, the state DOTs ends up interacting extensively with regional and local jurisdictions in the distribution of funds and in the design of projects. If governments at every level have complete streets policies, it can smooth the way toward agreement on specific design treatments.

Metropolitan Planning Organizations, with their critical role of disbursing federal transportation dollars, almost always focus their complete streets efforts on how to better select projects to fund. They have been leaders in creating project selection checklists and scoring systems that include multimodal criteria. They can accelerate implementation by requiring local governments to think through the needs of all users in project requests. MPOs also play an important educational role, holding workshops and writing handbooks and guides to help their members understand how to convert to a complete streets approach. But MPOs (and their cousins, rural planning organizations) take a back seat when it comes to making change on the ground; most do not actually build projects, so they are less likely to wade into creating design standards.

Local governments—counties, cities, townships, and other local bodies—are closest to the people who might be walking, bicycling, or taking the bus along their roads. But beyond that, it is impossible to generalize their approach because land use patterns, responsibility for road construction and maintenance, and their governing systems are so varied. Big cities like New York, San Francisco, and Chicago have the "good bones" of a pre-automobile street grid and robust transit systems that have allowed them to focus their efforts on ambitious long-term plans and innovative design solutions that reallocate street space to pedestrians, bicycle riders, and public transportation. And because they are more built out, they are not building new roads. The transportation agency and public works department may be able to focus on smaller retrofit projects to improve the existing road system amid infill and brownfield development.

In contrast, big cities and suburban counties where most development took place after World War II face a much different challenge. They must deal with hundreds of miles of relatively disconnected roads built only for car travel. Their initial efforts are likely to focus on triage, eliminating the most dangerous spots with retrofit sidewalks, bike lanes, and transit crossings. Progress will be slow, because so many streets need so much. Growth is another factor. Among cities and counties that are still physically expanding, private developers are major players because they are building new roads as they build houses, stores, and office buildings. In these places, the complete streets effort may focus first on changing subdivision regulations to require a complete streets approach (see later in this chapter). And if these places want to create more walkable neighborhoods, they will need to transform land use patterns and support better transit networks—both beyond the scope of a simple complete streets policy.

Political structure and staff capacity make a difference as well. In large cities, the mayor can use his executive function to work with agency leadership to direct sweeping change. These cities generally have significant internal capacity and are able to hire many specialized workers; if the leadership is on board, changing the practices of employees is relatively straightforward. Change may come fairly quickly, but leaders still need to work hard to break down barriers and improve communication between departments.

In most counties and small cities, elected officials play a different role. They are purposely separated from the day-to-day workings of their jurisdictions; professional managers are hired to administer county or city business. In this case, the policy makers have a limited ability to ensure effective implementation, but they still play an important role (as a county board member from Arlington, Virginia, discusses in chapter 6). Many smaller cities and towns also tend to hire out much of the transportation work to consultants, who typically have a more traditional approach to road construction. That means these jurisdictions need to write requests for proposals in a new way that spells out the new approach. Small towns may not build any of their own roads; nonetheless, a few have successfully used complete streets policies to push county and state agencies to change their construction plans on roads through their jurisdictions. Decatur, Georgia, and tiny Battle Lake, Minnesota, are notable for this approach.

These variations reveal that when it comes to changing how decisions are made, it is not just one system that needs to change but a range of systems developed and controlled by different agencies. Chapter 4 focused on how transportation planning departments—the agencies that plan and orchestrate road improvements—are changing their approach. But just about everywhere, a full commitment to creating safe roads for all users requires stepping out of transportation planning to address the big picture of what developers are building, as well as the incremental work of maintaining the current transportation system.

Achieving Complete Streets by Regulating Private Development

Many communities are changing systems outside of transportation planning that affect the street and the way people use it, such as zoning ordinances and subdivision regulations. In many communities, transportation facilities are built primarily by developers in the course of building subdivisions and commercial buildings; typically, they are also required to improve roads surrounding the development.

Many communities are changing land use regulations to make them more pedestrian friendly. They are changing their zoning codes to require developers to put parking in back and to provide more street connections. This will assist complete streets implementation efforts, and the transportation agency may pay closer attention to ensuring that street infrastructure matches the surrounding context.

In some places, developers are already successfully building more compact, walkable communities, and they can become allies: these developers want to build more connected streets with less parking. But in much of the United States, the norm is still to build disconnected office parks and isolated subdivisions that rely on automobile travel. Developers may resist changes to development codes, and without new code language the jurisdiction may be unable to require compliance.

When Matt Dyrdahl worked as a regional planner in Bemidji in north-central Minnesota, he found this out the hard way. Working under the region's Active Living collaboration, Dyrdahl had helped shepherd through multimodal changes to the regional transportation and land use plan, as well as the park and trails plan. He had also helped get an Active Living resolution through city council affirming support for complete streets. One of the first tests was a request to a developer rebuilding an appliance store; he was asked to include a paved trail along the roadway to provide access to a school. When the conditional use permit for the development came before the Joint Planning Board, which Matthew chaired, he gave what he felt was a compelling opening to the discussion. He argued for the health and safety benefits of the side path, and many at the meeting nodded. But then, he recalls, "one of the landowners, a member of a powerful local family, got up. He said safety is good, but there is nothing in the zoning ordinance to compel us to do this." Another planning board member made a motion saying the policy didn't apply, and the paved path was quickly voted down. "That was it. I was so irate," remembers Matthew. He went home that night and started writing a revision of the zoning code; part of his revision redefined the street from "a way for vehicular traffic" to "a strip of land used or intended to be used for the passage or travel of motor vehicles, non-motorized vehicles and pedestrians." The developer did eventually agree to build a path, but it was not paved.

Matthew later learned to follow the lead of a colleague, senior planner Mitzi Baker at the Rochester/Olmsted planning department. She has focused Rochester's implementation efforts around changing every possible document, under the theory that the more thoroughly complete streets is embedded, the harder it will be to remove. When working for community approval of new subdivision regulations, she and her staff brought developers on board by sitting down with them and applying the proposed changes to a few pending development proposals to work through the potential ramifications.

In Charlotte, changes to the zoning codes were the most difficult phase of institutionalizing complete streets. The staff had expanded the city's visionary Transportation Action Plan into the award-winning Urban Street Design Guidelines. But the process stalled for a while as the planners worked to build support for new ordinances to guide developers in street design, street connectivity, tree planting, and orienting development to transit. Developers resisted new subdivision standards that would require sidewalks and more street connectivity. The Charlotte DOT conducted an analysis that found that the cost of adding sidewalks would be insignificant for developers who were already doing major earth moving. The analysis also found that building more frequent street connections would result in a 10 to 20 percent increase in space devoted to streets—far less than some had feared, and a portion that the city council found acceptable.[5] The council adopted the standards and the other ordinances aimed at creating complete streets. Now the city is working on an ordinance to apply to the installation of traffic-calming measures.

Some communities also use "adequate public facilities" or "concurrency" ordinances that require developers to build enough road or sewer infrastructure to serve the growth their development will bring. Prince George's County, Maryland, a suburb of Washington, DC, has long required developers to provide for new automobile traffic by installing traffic lights or widening roads. In 2012, the city council amended its subdivision code to require developers to provide adequate bicycle and pedestrian facilities within a half mile of their project; the new code also encourages transit-oriented design.

The city of Nashville decided some years ago to require zero-lot-line development to phase out new buildings set back behind parking lots. Ironically, planners say that is now presenting a problem. Now, when the city would like a few more feet for sidewalks and bicycle lanes, developers see it as an infringement on their right to develop right to the edge of their property. The city is working to make another adjustment to the code to solve this problem and is not backing off on new zoning regulations—Nashville has adopted a new urbanist–inspired Form-Based Code for its downtown, as well as other "Overlay Districts" that make it easier for developers to build compact, walkable centers and neighborhoods.[6]

Achieving Complete Streets through Maintenance and Operations

Turning to maintenance as a first step in complete streets implementation can accelerate change, gradually build support for bigger investments, and become the centerpiece of a complete streets transformation. This may seem counterintuitive: many jurisdictions exempt maintenance projects from their complete streets policies, fearing that they would be obliged to turn every resurfacing into an expensive project to achieve a perfect multimodal street. The request for an exemption provision is often made by a public works department that already feels under siege, with too many roads to maintain with too little money.

Indeed, maintenance of the nation's road infrastructure has become a crisis. The American Association of State Highway Transportation Officials (AASHTO) estimates that one third of major urban roads are in poor condition.[7] Yet, little money is dedicated specifically to maintenance and repair. The federal transportation law passed in 2012 rolled the established bridge repair program into a new and broader National Highway Performance Program. FHWA has classified 69,223 bridges as structurally deficient.[8] Many states have continued to devote a majority of their dollars to new road projects, leaving less than half the funding to take care of 99 percent of the system.[9] A few states are changing this with asset management programs that seek to more systematically keep roads in a state of good repair, and the federal program is moving toward making states more accountable for repairing roads.

In many cities and states, routine maintenance is handled by a wholly different department than transportation improvements. The public works department usually takes on filling potholes and resurfacing streets, doing so on its own schedule and with its own budget, leadership, and institutional culture. The everyday concerns of public works engineers are frequently left out of the conversation among transportation planners about lofty long-term goals.

As a result, many jurisdictions look on maintenance obligations as a barrier to achieving complete streets. They end up backing into the realization that maintenance projects can be a tremendous asset. This was the case in Salt Lake City, Utah. Planners and citizens had put together a bicycle master plan in 2004 that designated corridors to create a bicycle network using standard bike lanes and designated bike routes. Progress had been slow. In 2010, without much fanfare, the city converted an earlier Complete Streets Executive Order to an ordinance. The policy document is weak, but political will has been strong under Mayor Ralph Becker, and maintenance turned into a key that finally unlocked change for the city's streets.

In 2010, bicycle and pedestrian coordinator Becka Roolf got a call from someone on a maintenance team in the Streets Division about a road getting a slurry seal, a very thin fresh coat of asphalt. He asked her, "Do you want bike lanes?" She said yes, but she was dismayed when he replied, "Okay, we're doing it in three weeks!" There simply wasn't the time to come up with a new striping plan and get community feedback. But the experience helped Roolf see the potential for future projects, and she gave herself a crash course in understanding the process and schedule for slurry- and chip-sealing roadways. The public works department started to give her more notice, but not much. "It was always a scramble to get them designed and to hold a community meeting. We were really working week by week," she says. She and the public works officials relied on the complete streets ordinance more than on the 2004 bike plan. Following the complete streets approach, they looked for space on every project, which was not too hard to find on Salt Lake's famously wide streets. By the end of the paving season in 2011, Salt Lake City had added nearly fifty miles of bike lanes and marked shared lanes, mainly through the annual budget for the pavement management system. In the same year, the number of people commuting by bicycle in the city rose by 27 percent—and it held at this level in 2012.

Seizing such opportunities can make a difference right away. Maintenance projects offer an avenue to transform streets that can be efficient, less controversial, and quick. This is important because the systemic, internal changes that are essential to long-term success are largely invisible to the general public. Citizens, advocates, and political leaders who helped get a complete streets policy adopted want to see change on the ground—now. But practitioners may look at the hundreds of miles of incomplete streets and not know where to begin. Money for big projects has usually been allocated years in advance, and some projects may be too far along to redesign. Reworking master plans, strategic plans, and capital improvement programs takes time and resources. Maintenance projects are a way for a city to jump-start its complete streets commitment.

A small example comes from Illinois, where Cook County told the City of Des Plaines that Mt. Prospect Road bordering the city would soon be repaved. Des Plaines had a complete streets policy in place and had identified the road for improvement in its 2011 Active Transportation Plan. So, city engineers asked for bike lanes; Cook County has a policy too, so agreement came easily. Advocates estimate that without this coordination, the city would have had to wait another five years for the pavement markings.[10]

Jurisdictions of all sizes now recognize the importance of using maintenance and operations work to quicken the pace of a complete streets transformation. The Sacramento Area Council of Governments now requires that cities and counties that want federal funding for road rehabilitation projects include improvements for all users. The North Carolina Department of Transportation's complete streets guidelines also make a strong case for maintenance and operations projects as a key component in the state's approach.[11] The guidelines clarify that the biggest challenges are timing and coordination. Word of upcoming paving projects needs to be shared with local jurisdictions and transit agencies that have their own plans for the corridor, and with other interested parties, such as a complete streets advisory committee. And the information needs to be shared early enough for changes to be made and approved.

Thinking through the maintenance process ahead of time can avoid a mad scramble like the one that Roolf experienced in Salt Lake City. In Hennepin County, Minnesota, the pavement preservation system rehabilitates about one hundred lane miles per year, but members of the bicycle advisory committee say a lack of communication led to missed opportunities. So the public works department restructured the program to make it more responsive and collaborative. The county has set up three maintenance funds with different purposes and timelines. Immediate pavement repair will be covered by emergency funds. The "overlay funding program" will look out two to three years and will support changes within the curb line, such as crosswalks and bike lanes. The new "Pavement Preservation Plus" program will expand paving projects to include such changes as adding pedestrian bump-outs and sidewalk repair and installation (but draws the line at any underground work). The programs with longer timelines will allow the bicycle advisory committee and many other stakeholders more time and information to help ensure these projects miss no opportunities.

Don Reid, the paving/right-of-way manager in Nashville, Tennessee, went to a Complete Streets Workshop and was urged by director of healthy living initiatives Adetokunbo "Toks" Omishakin to find a way to incorporate changes into his projects. He thought it was a good idea. "From my standpoint, I'm already out there in the roadway as a paving manager," says Reid. "I'm already touching everything in that road." He created a complete streets checklist that collects the information needed to determine what improvements can be made as part of paving projects. Since then, his projects have widened paved shoulders, narrowed automobile lanes to add bike lanes, and added sharrows (pavement markings that indicate a shared bicycle/auto lane). One of his big challenges is decades' worth of storm water grates installed with parallel slots that catch bicycle wheels. The public works department can't change every grate right away, so Reid says they now require that anyone who digs up the road has to make storm water grates in the vicinity bike friendly. That includes entities such as the city water department, Piedmont Gas, and the Nashville Electric Service. Reid's work has little to do with the sophisticated new street typologies created by the planning department and included in the new Major Collector and Street Plan, but it helps make the city safer nonetheless.

Agencies can also improve the travel environment by attending to the operation of the road system, particularly at intersections. Jurisdictions can adjust signal timing and replace old pedestrian signal heads with new countdown signals (generally speaking, shorter light cycles work better

Pedestrian and bicycle safety improvements at an expanded intersection in Charlotte. (Photos courtesy Mecklenburg County and Pictometry International.)

for pedestrians). Systems that allow buses to trip lights or hold a green light can dramatically reduce bus delay. Agencies can also install loop detectors in the pavement so bicycles can get a green light, and audible signals for people with impaired sight. The North Carolina guidebook includes a list of potential operations improvements projects that help create complete streets.[12] It also includes technical recommendations from the NCDOT maintenance and operations staff to ensure success, such as coordinating road conversions with new signal timing.

The Value of Incremental Change

While maintenance and operations projects allow change to begin to happen right away, they also have value precisely because they are pedestrian in the first sense of the word. In Anniston Alabama, city councilman Jay Jenkins told the *Anniston Star* that the city's new complete streets policy would be "a plodding kind of change." The initial changes made to complete the streets can be modest and unimaginative, but within this drudgery lies the makings of metamorphosis.

A new in-road pedestrian sign or a curb ramp on a suburban arterial are small things. But when it comes to safer streets, the divine is in the details, because these elements introduce the human scale into the road environment. For a wheelchair user, that curb ramp can mean the difference between independent travel and reliance on expensive and inconvenient paratransit service. As the small details proliferate, they start to telegraph a new message about the road: the people alighting from buses or bicycling down the street have a place, and they need to be seen and respected by drivers.

FHWA has issued a primer to help agencies achieve sustainability through maintenance and operations.[13] It includes a guide for incorporating multimodal factors into an operations plan for a typical major suburban arterial over a fifteen-year period. The primer makes clear that such an arterial—with its wide lanes, many driveways, and few safe crossings—won't be transformed overnight. But it can be transformed nonetheless. According to the timeline, in year 2, safety projects concentrate on fixing a critical intersection or improving intersections for people with disabilities. In year 4, a new corridor access management plan enables the agency to close some driveways and add sidewalks. By year 7, land use changes and improvements in earlier years allow the agency to reconfigure the street for six lanes of traffic instead of eight, with a landscaped median and continuous bike lanes; a roundabout may follow the next year. By year 12, it is time to start up bus rapid transit (BRT), with signal prioritization, stations with prepaid boarding, and stops with signs that tell when the next bus is coming.[14] This gradual method is how most of the nation's suburban arterials will likely become complete streets.

Incremental changes are especially valuable in communities like Anniston, where driving is the default. Small changes can fulfill obvious safety needs, such as lowering speeds through neighborhoods and providing a place to walk. Achieving a minimum level of safety is a threshold over which most communities must pass before they can start to realize any health, sustainability or economic goals that depend on getting more people out on foot, bicycle, or bus. Modest changes build understanding and support, and also allow time for people to change their habits so the new sidewalks, bike lanes, and bus shelters are well used. Indeed, the *Anniston Star*'s editorial board praised the move, concluding that "cities that invest in tangible, quality-of-life amenities are investing in their future." Gradual change can also lead to a gradual realization that a few bike lanes won't be enough to really transform a community—and that can lead to more far-reaching projects and plans. Complete streets can become a "gateway drug" to smarter growth.

The Ability to Think Big

If a community has a strong commitment, maintenance projects can become a route to making systematic changes within existing budgets. This is because every road needs to be maintained, and as each road is systematically touched in the maintenance schedule, it can be improved to better serve all users. A common technique to do this is a systematic application of road conversions.

Colorado Springs, Colorado, has reconfigured many streets with its maintenance budget by converting roads when they come up for repaving. Before the economic downturn, the city repaved 7 to 10 percent of its network every year; the pace has since slowed to about 3 percent a year. The city made a decision to use the opportunity to systematically convert a significant number of its roads to eliminate through or turn lanes and make space for bicycle lanes. The conversions are also a technique used to control speed in neighborhoods, because they narrow lanes and prevent passing. An early conversion on Cheyenne Boulevard showed that before the conversion, most drivers were traveling at forty-one miles per hour (mph) on the thirty-five mph road; bringing it down to two automobile lanes with a center turn lane brought average speeds down to between thirty-six and thirty-nine mph. One early "diet" ran into trouble when county commissioners saw city workers installing it in front of the county government headquarters; then–transportation planner Kristin Bennett says reducing lanes was simply "not seen as progress" by the commissioners. But over time, the conversions have become routine enough that in most neighborhoods the city announces them by letter. If the project includes plantings, the letter offers residents the chance to pick trees to be planted in front of their house. The projects are popular, and residents appreciate the direct communication.

Bennett says she would like to coordinate all street construction projects through the city's construction management software so no opportunity is missed. She gives the example of the installation of a midblock trail crossing near a school: "The guy who is managing concrete contracts over at Streets, he doesn't know what I want for schools. And it shouldn't be reliant on him hoping he knows me, and giving me a phone call and saying, 'what do you want?' It should just" –she snaps her fingers—"pop up in the systems we spend a lot of time and money on."

A Prominent Place for Public Works

Focusing on maintenance projects can also help resolve two other barriers to complete streets: the perceived lack of funding and the division between planning and public works staff.

As mentioned earlier, maintenance faces a funding crisis. It may be difficult to build political support to allocate sufficient money for the uninspiring work of maintaining roads exactly as they are now. But what if maintenance projects can be billed as a method to achieve popular complete streets? They can draw more support. Case in point: Hennepin County's board approved a new allocation of $500,000 for its new "Pavement Preservation Plus" program. Advocates can also become allies for increasing funding for strapped transportation agencies, if the advocates can see a commitment to using all dollars to improve the roadways for all users. In La Crosse, Wisconsin, bicycle advocates and planners who want complete streets are also supporting an overall increase in the public works departments' budget, in part to help implement the city's new bike plan. The strategy could also work on the federal level. An annual opinion survey taken to gauge national support for increased gas taxes finds that more specific proposals draw more support: while the survey does not ask about complete streets, the two options receiving over 50 percent support in the latest survey were proposed taxes dedicated to maintenance and to safety projects.[15]

Incorporating improvements into maintenance also gives this often unimaginative work a whiff of vision and excitement and can help build bonds between planners and public works staff. When Arlington, Virginia, was first striping bike lanes, Charlie Denney, the bicycle/pedestrian program manager, had struck up a good relationship with the manager of the striping crews in the Engineering and Operations office. One Monday morning, Denney says he picked up a phone message left by the manager on Saturday: "Charlie, you've gotta call me first thing Monday, something happened this weekend that's never happened to me before!" Denney knew the crews had been working overtime on the weekend putting in new bike lanes, so he braced for the worst. But when he called back, he says the manager reported, "We were out there [striping] on Military Road, coming up the hill by 30th Street, and a family was standing out there and they were *cheering* for us! Nobody in my work has ever cheered for me! It made my day!" Denney says, "He had been pretty good to work with, but after that, it was a true partnership. He would look for places to put bike lanes."

It turns out that the "plodding kind of change" offered by maintenance-oriented complete streets projects are not only an efficient way to create safer streets but can also become a key to securing long-term support for multimodal roads. It can also break down the cultural divide between planners who spend most of their time drawing up long-range plans and engineers who are busy working on the streets every day.

Ultimately, success usually depends less on what gets done but on how complete streets proponents go about doing it. This is the subject of chapter 6.

Nashville Mayor Karl Dean signs the city's complete streets policy while staff, including Adetokunbo "Toks" Omishakin, director of healthy living initiatives, look on. (Photo by Gary Layda, City of Nashville.)

CHAPTER SIX

Practitioners as Champions

A FTER WE STARTED THE National Complete Streets Coalition, I spent a lot of time developing a series of focused fact sheets that brought together the best and most specific answers we could find on every topic related to complete streets. The website was soon overflowing with reports and resources on every aspect of the benefits of complete streets. But somehow they were never enough. They never slaked the hunger from people around the country for very specific information about how to answer a challenging question with an indisputable fact. Over time, I realized I was learning how to overcome barriers not by regurgitating facts but by hearing stories about how others had made change happen.[1]

The tendency of engineers, advocates, and policy makers—of most people, in fact—is to see change as a rational exercise, with facts driving action. Complete streets are safer streets, and they have plenty of other benefits too. Shouldn't that be enough? Missing from this equation is the way humans make decisions, change habits, and become infused with a new sense of purpose.

This chapter is about how advocates of complete streets, and particularly those who work inside agencies, navigate these murkier waters. It is about how they come to understand power structures and work to institutionalize complete streets in their agencies, not simply by providing facts or creating new street cross sections but by building relationships, giving colleagues a visceral understanding of a multimodal streetscape, and helping broaden ownership of a complete streets approach.

This is the work of a complete streets champion. I've encountered these champions over and over again, and their techniques, personalities, and job titles vary widely. What they all have in common is a clarity of purpose, a determination to find a way to remove, soften, or get around obstacles to achieve that purpose, and an ability to bring others along. Champions do not have to be well-known, high-powered officials, although the movement certainly has those as well: Gabe Klein of Washington, DC, and Chicago and Janette Sadik-Kahn of New York are celebrated for their roles as champions, transforming not only the departments they lead but their entire cities. Since most people will never reach their level, this book focuses on champions of more modest stature who succeed in driving change inside their agencies, often without holding an official position of influence.

And while the term "champion" may imply one person leading a charge, true success usually means that many champions are operating and that they are succeeding in getting change institutionalized so it will persist after they leave. For example, in New Jersey, consultants, advocates, the state bicycle-pedestrian coordinator, a small-town mayor, and the head of the Department of Transportation are all championing complete streets— using their particular skills and networks to reframe the issue, take their colleagues down a new path, and persuade others to join in.

Profile of a Champion

The first complete streets champion I got to know was Michael Ronkin. At the time, he was the bicycle and pedestrian program manager for the Oregon Department of Transportation, and our first encounter was an argument over the phone about pedestrian safety statistics. The content doesn't matter here, but Michael's response does: rather than shutting me out, he proposed we co-present a session about the issue at the upcoming Pro-Bike conference in 2000 in Philadelphia. I agreed, and we've been working together ever since; after he became a consultant, we ended up driving all over Virginia, developing the first version of the Complete Streets Workshop.

Michael's shock of thick black hair matches his direct style; he has an uncanny ability to include his underlying philosophy when answering any question. He grew up in Geneva, Switzerland; it isn't his wisp of an accent that gives him away, but his orientation toward what he calls a "sensible transportation system." When he went to work for the Oregon

Department of Transportation (ODOT) in 1989, it didn't make sense to him that his department spent an inordinate amount of time preparing a report to document that the agency was spending the required 1 percent of its funds on bicycle and pedestrian projects. The state's so-called Bike Bill, passed in 1974, had made this the law; as the nation's first proto-complete streets policy, it also required that "Footpaths and bicycle trails, including curb cuts or ramps . . . shall be provided wherever a highway, road or street is being constructed, reconstructed or relocated." Yet, little attention had been paid to this "routine accommodation" part of the stat-ute. Exceptions were routinely granted, and sidewalks were not included on state projects unless local governments wanted and paid for them.

Right away, Ronkin demonstrated one attribute of a champion: in-stead of grumbling about the uselessness of the spending report, he found a way around it. He told me, "When I became the program manager, I just stopped publishing the report [on how much we'd spent], and waited for any complaints. Guess when the first knock came? Never. No one gave a s--t about those reports." This freed up his time to follow the directive of his new boss, Bill Geibel, who wanted to get serious about implementing the routine accommodation part of the law. Their first strategy: getting a series of opinions from the state attorney general confirming that the law did indeed require bike and pedestrian facilities, on both state DOT and local transportation projects.

Ronkin did not rely on legal rulings alone: he built relationships with people who could help him advance the goal. He sought out the help of people in the department with more experience and more credibility. He befriended Terry Wheeler, the official in the design section who was re-sponsible for granting exceptions to the policy, as well as another employ-ee responsible for standard drawings. The Americans with Disabilities Act was coming into force at the time, and Ronkin says, "We kind of hijacked ADA to help enforce our walkway standards." ODOT formed a working group of ten cities and counties to develop ADA standards. "The cities were grateful, they were scrambling, because they didn't have the staff and resources to develop their own standards," says Ronkin. Oregon ended up with some of the strongest walkway standards in the nation—including an end to the requirement that cities pay for them on state projects.

As the standards went into effect, Ronkin worked closely with

Wheeler and project managers who were seeking exceptions, and their fear dissipated. "They were stunned at how often we agreed with them on one of the exceptions," says Ronkin. The state law allowed exceptions when there was no need for facilities, when they would be too costly, and when they would compromise safety. Ronkin says that after working with Wheeler for a few years, he was consulted on exceptions only one or two times a year. "Which meant project managers were doing their jobs, which is ultimately what we want out of complete streets policies," he says. "Ninety-nine percent of the time they were making the right decisions."

ODOT already had a pretty inclusive decision-making process, with a tradition of working through committees, and Ronkin used the process to maximum effect. The law had created a bicycle committee, which became a bicycle/pedestrian committee under his watch and helped give credibility to his work. To reach practitioners across the state, he presented at the quarterly meetings of regional managers. Although he wasn't invited, his boss was, so it was easy to get on the agenda. The two of them used the process to introduce and work through the new walkway standards. But even then, not everyone was convinced. Ronkin and Geibel were able to rely on the strength of the Oregon statute, reaffirmed by the rulings they had attained, to get serious about the exceptions clause. A test case came up when one of the regions that had been particularly resistant didn't include a sidewalk on a highway reconstruction project. Ronkin recounts, "[This road had] one of these classic goat trails in the grass. How could you say it meets the exception? We wouldn't let the project go through, and that shook everyone up."

While Ronkin was able to rely on the strength of the state law in that instance, his own resume did not convey authority: Ronkin is not a trained engineer; his college degree is in agronomy. Yet, his stature in the department became such that he was routinely invited to serve on relevant committees. When the state undertook a rewrite of its design manual in 1999, he was asked to write several sections. When I asked him whether he felt qualified, he recounted a piece of advice Geibel gave him that he has used throughout his career: "Don't look at a person's title or position; find out if that person is effective, and if so, glom on to that person." He worked with other people who had credibility and so developed his own.

He also noted that he was never in a management position. "But my title was 'Manager.' They didn't know the bicycle and pedestrian program was just two people. It came across that I was important." In short, "I bluffed."

He even bluffed a bit when it came to including facilities for bicycles and pedestrians in maintenance projects, which is not covered by the 1974 statute. He knew that overlay projects were a huge opportunity to make improvements, so he worked with Terry Wheeler to create a new policy that clarified what should happen in these projects, elevating the priority placed on closing gaps in the pedestrian and bikeway network. It wasn't a perfect fix, but it helped.

Ronkin's story reveals several attributes of champions and the tactics they have used to make changes in transportation planning and design. He used the change tenets outlined in chapter 1: he helped reframe the organizational mission, worked to define a clear path of change to follow, and did so not only through focusing on technical specifications but by building a power base and building relationships and buy-in. He does not shrink back from conflict, and now, as a consultant, he embraces the chance to make change by connecting with people on a personal level as he teaches workshops around the country. He says: "It is one person at a time. It is that ah-ha moment when you've made a difference. What's important is making that eye contact, seeing the body language, how that moment [of change] is visible. They come up to you in a break at the workshop and say, 'you made me think differently about what I do.' It's very personal. That's only possible by going out in the field and talking, talking, talking."

Activities and Attitudes of Champions

Champions generally start with an activity discussed in chapter 4: gaining a full understanding of the way decisions are made. A recent federal report is full of case studies of communities that have taken a complete streets approach. *Local Policies and Practices That Support Safe Pedestrian Environments* concludes that success "has largely been driven by the ability of those involved . . . to make accurate and clear assessment of the institutional, political, or financial framework at play and adopt a practical approach that fits within that framework."[2] Gil Peñalosa, who helped his brother Enrique with the transformation of Bogotá, Colombia, in the late 1990s and went on to found the group 8-80 Cities, calls these people "doers"—people with a clear vision who don't just throw up their hands when they come to a barrier but instead seek to understand the root of the problem and then change it.

In California, Chris Ratekin, who oversees the implementation of Caltrans's complete streets policy, Deputy Directive 64, says all the new policies, guidance, and manuals are well and good—but then you have to look at why change still isn't happening. She says that requires sitting down with other agency staff and working through the details. "I can't solve all the problems because I come into it with my planning expertise," she says. "It takes those front-line people, the staff who are in the weeds in those programs, to be able to have those ah-ha perceptions" on how their work must change to meet new multimodal objectives.

This is where inclusive decision making really begins—getting more and more people to feel ownership of complete streets, so they can tackle their part of making it a reality. Developing a commitment to a complete streets approach among elected officials or practitioners may begin with giving them facts or research that helps allay fears about costs or safety problems. But it is essential to cement a sense of ownership, and that happens through personal experience.

Seattle's Peter Lagerwey, who told the story of the surprise inside the Seattle DOT when residents all chose to use neighborhood transportation funds on bicycle and pedestrian improvements, explains why his colleagues were surprised. He says when the city started on its path toward multimodal roads, all but two of the midlevel managers inside SDOT lived in suburban areas outside the city. They simply brought their autocentric biases to their jobs, at least until they really listened to what residents wanted. Over time, SDOT began to hire more employees who lived in the city.

Similarly, James Simpson, the head of the New Jersey DOT, says he came into his job with "the perspective of a motorist." But he recounts his transformation into a pedestrian after moving into a walkable neighborhood in Trenton: "As a pedestrian, I've seen drivers speeding down local streets, showing a lack of regard for pedestrians and bicyclists. I see the need for more 'Complete Streets'— more and improved sidewalks; better markings at crosswalks to put motorists on alert; bike paths where needed; and intersection improvements, including countdown pedestrian signals and accessible curb cuts at crosswalks to accommodate those who are mobility impaired." [3]

Moving to a new neighborhood, as James Simpson did, is not necessary to gain this visceral understanding; champions can help develop it in political leaders, practitioners, and citizens no matter where they live. Dan Burden and Mark Fenton qualify as mega-champions of complete streets; they both travel the country speaking to community leaders, showing them compelling photographs, and most importantly, taking people out for a walk. They are both champions of using walking audits to help everyone see and understand deficiencies. [4]

Saint Louis Park, Minnesota, brought Fenton in to conduct a "Winter Walking Tour" for both elected officials and transportation agency workers. He led the group on a walk down snowy city streets so everyone could experience the barriers presented by mounds of snow that block access to buses or reduce sight lines, and slick surfaces that imperil older pedestrians. During warmer weather, the city sponsored a bike tour, taking council and key department leaders out on principal bike routes. Both events built a common experience of what it is actually like to be out on the streets of their city without a car. The city council continues to refer back to the experience during its deliberations. The Michigan DOT has formalized this approach statewide with a program called "Training Wheels." It starts with classroom instruction on the AASHTO bikeway design guidelines. But it then puts traffic engineers, planners, and elected officials onto bikes to ride around their town—to experience good bike lanes, bad streets, and ugly intersections.

Complete Streets Workshop instructor Mike Dannemiller, a consultant in New Jersey, brings a wheelchair along at every workshop he gives and always takes attendees out to navigate a sloping sidewalk. "The wheelchair is more valuable than all the talk in the world for giving workshop attendees a memorable experience," he says. "These big strong guys discover they can't make the wheelchair go straight!" Suddenly, the need to minimize the cross slope at driveways has a whole new meaning.

Not everyone will be convinced. But complete streets champions tend not to be too bothered by the presence of opponents. They focus more on building support than on countering opposition. Opponents do demand attention; the *Local Practices* report discusses opposition from citizens, developers, partnering entities, and internal agency sources. All of these players have an investment in the status quo. Their presence should not be a surprise, but it draws energy and attention. The opposition provokes anxiety, and complete streets boosters want to do something to make it go away. But a focus on answering the objections of opponents is generally not an effective advocacy strategy. Facts won't be enough to win them all over. And in answering their questions, advocates often end up inside the opponents' traditional frame of reference. Champions can choose an easier road: they can assert the new frame of complete streets, identify more receptive people in the community, nurture them, and build a power base. They can seek out specific supporters to counter negative voices. Over time, the opponents, who once loomed so large, will seem less relevant. More people will speak in support of the concept—and will be willing to engage in discussions with the opponents. And if the opponents hear the right message from the right people, many of them will slowly, slowly, come to understand and embrace complete streets.

Most importantly, champions build relationships, constantly broadening their network of supporters. The movement's diverse base means supporters can come from just about anywhere. Three basic types of supporters deserve wooing: citizens, community leaders, and practitioners.

Engaging Citizens

Curiously, one of the biggest untapped assets in many complete streets implementation efforts is the support of citizens and the general public. In most cases, complete streets policy adoption has been sparked by citizen advocacy—bicycle advocacy groups, AARP state offices, and smart growth groups have all launched multiple successful policy adoption campaigns. The public health push for complete streets has in large part been sustained by organizing many constituencies to push lawmakers for change. But when it comes to the "professional" task of implementation, many practitioners fail to reach out and use that broad base of public support.

Transportation professionals have grown wary of traditional public input; they are used to a "design-and-defend" dynamic, in which public involvement meetings mostly mean being pummeled by citizens unhappy with plans or projects. Citizens distrust transportation and planning agencies with good reason; in the past, transportation "improvements" frequently meant a degradation of their neighborhood as roads got wider and faster. Some residents may also hold the prevalent views that the top transportation planning priority should be easing their automobile commute, or that sidewalks destroy the "rural" character of their subdivision and bring in "unwanted elements."

The problem is compounded when a resident's first introduction to the complete streets concept comes at a meeting about a project on their own block. New techniques make streets look different, and unfamiliar features, such as traffic calming measures, can provoke consternation despite their clear safety advantages. Drivers may chafe as speeding becomes more difficult, and most controversial are projects that directly reallocate road space, such as a road conversion that reduces automobile lanes, or a project that would remove automobile parking in order to provide for a bicycle lane.

Early attempts to add sidewalks and bike lanes in Duluth, Minnesota, ran into plenty of resistance—fears that roads would be too wide and too costly. Property owners had a direct stake in the outcome, because individual homeowners surrounding a road project are assessed for 25 percent of its cost. Without a strong base of understanding of the overall community goals of complete streets, residents were asked at early meetings to vote on what a street should include—and promptly voted down features for nonmotorized users. They used those early meetings to take ownership of multimodal projects and oppose them—ignoring any wider network benefit or new community goals they were intended to serve.

When the focus is at the project level, you can bet that opponents, often characterized as NIMBYs (for "Not In My Backyard"), will turn up. They are energized by what they view as an immediate threat and will come to meetings, make calls, and write letters, blog posts, and tweets. But while many citizens may think the changes are fine, they won't be motivated to speak up—unless they already feel a connection to the project's bigger goals or to a group supporting the project.

That's why it is essential for agencies to build confidence and more generalized support for the complete streets concept before it gets to the project level. Proponents need to nurture supportive interest groups and individuals in the community as assets for the long haul. These nonprofessionals have a big advantage over practitioners steeped in years of training—they don't think of street projects in separate silos, and they immediately understand and embrace the view that street projects should serve everyone. And city council will listen to them. Complete streets proponents inside agencies who can identify and develop relationships with community champions will find them invaluable as projects that look different begin to roll out. They can provide essential, positive reinforcement when those resisting change turn out in force at community meetings. Community champions can be identified during the complete streets policy adoption process, and their support can be nurtured directly with ongoing contact and e-mail updates about projects. Agencies can keep building support with presentations, short videos, and websites that explain the local benefits of complete streets policies and what types of projects to expect.

More and more practitioners and agencies are discovering that documenting public support provides a powerful foundation for change that extends beyond policy adoption. National, state, and local polls show strong support for policies that create a more multimodal transportation infrastructure. Local funding measures for public transportation have a strong record of success. In 2012, more than two thirds of proposed ballot measures across the country passed (and two that gained 65 percent support failed due to California's supermajority requirement[5]). A recent nationwide public opinion poll found that 59 percent of Americans want more transportation options so they don't have to drive everywhere—and that 63 percent are in favor of addressing traffic congestion by improving public transportation and developing communities where people do not have to drive so much.[6] Only one in five favored road building as the primary congestion-fighting strategy.

When I cite national figures, people in a town I'm visiting will tell me, "We're different around here—we really love our cars." But public attitudes about transportation are shifting all across the United States, and state or locally focused polls provide even more compelling evidence of support. The Missouri Department of Transportation's public opinion poll has asked residents if they agreed with a proposal to spend up to 25 percent of a transportation project's budget on facilities for walking, bicycling, and riding public transportation—even if that means a reduction in the total number of projects that could be built. In 2008 and 2009, 47 percent of Missourians supported that statement; in 2010, 53 percent agreed. In Dallas, a Sunbelt, automobile-dependent city, a 2011 poll found that 85 percent of respondents were willing to give up at least a small portion of street space now devoted to cars to make room for other options. Sixty-eight percent felt that the local economy would benefit from creating more walkable and bikeable streets. In Charlotte, frequent surveys of residents reliably show support for the city's well-established complete streets approach. In 2010, an overwhelming 80 percent of respondents supported creating streets that accommodate all users, including motorists, pedestrians, bicyclists, and transit users.[7]

The Nashville regional planning agency laid the groundwork for its shift to a complete streets approach with a survey that found 90 percent of respondents get to work by driving alone.[8] When they were asked about the most important transportation problems to solve, a lack of options for transit, bicycling, and walking, along with poorly planned development, came out on top. The region translated that clear public support into a changed project-selection process that gave multimodal projects an edge, as described in chapter 8.

Referring back to that public support can help advance more mundane implementation challenges. In San Diego, the first regional routine accommodation policy was a single sentence contained in a bond measure passed by voters. Stephan Vance, on staff at the San Diego Association of Governments (SANGAG), worked with a team to develop strong rules for implementing the policy, proposing a matrix that clarified what types of facilities would be required for urban highways, transit projects, urban streets, collector streets of higher and lower design speeds, local streets, and rural roadways. Some elected officials expressed reservations, but Vance just kept coming back to the fact that the rules were carrying out a measure approved by a large majority of voters. This helped convince them to support it. A poll of residents taken a few years later confirmed the rules are expressing the will of the people: 79 percent of them supported creation of walkable neighborhoods as a greenhouse gas reduction strategy.

Another method for building public support is to start with noncontroversial projects and to reach out to especially dedicated constituencies.

I always recommend that jurisdictions new to complete streets steer clear of early projects that would require removing parking. Opposition is sure to arise, and suddenly the term *complete streets* has a negative association. Instead, pick projects that everyone can support.

Building and focusing public support is the stock-in-trade for advocacy groups, and advocates and practitioners work in tandem to sustain support for the changes required by a complete streets policy. This is the case in San Diego. Stephan Vance says that, early on, the only advocates were "cranky bicyclists," but that changed when Walk San Diego came on the scene in 1998. It was founded by Andy Hamilton, a planner at the San Diego Air Pollution Control District, and Vance credits him with the idea of going after political support to expand complete streets policies in the region and for engaging the mayor of San Diego. Walk San Diego has raised the profile of complete streets in the region by bringing in a range of educational and training opportunities and arranging with Vance to hold events at SANDAG's headquarters. They have brought in nationally recognized transportation experts for daylong workshops and forums and have arranged to use funds from a health grant to host two Complete Streets Workshops for agency staff, elected officials, and citizens from smaller jurisdictions adopting their own complete streets policies. Vance says of their work, "I used to feel I had to speak up personally but now more people are speaking up."

Hamilton has instilled a high degree of professionalism in the organization's advocacy strategy, a trend that is occurring nationwide. Kathleen Ferrier, Walk San Diego's policy manager, says, "Andy is so knowledgeable. He's not just pushing blindly for stuff; he recognizes, 'Okay, we have barriers and challenges, and we're going to help you work through those,' so it is more like a partnership. That set the platform for Walk San Diego." Ferrier coauthored two detailed, carefully researched reports on complete streets implementation in the region. *Safe for All*, a benchmark study of street design practices in the jurisdictions in the county, includes complete streets case studies and best practices from communities locally and across the country.[9] *From Policy to Pavement: Implementing Complete Streets in the San Diego Region* provides a full implementation toolbox and discussion of barriers for local communities.[10] Vance says that Hamilton and the staff at Walk San Diego are viewed as colleagues and they do good work—so they are hired as consultants when projects call for advancing the walking agenda. From Maine to New Mexico, nonprofit groups working for more walkable and bikeable communities and for more compact development provide expertise and services that can advance complete streets.

So what happened in Duluth, Minnesota, where residents had voted down improvements on their own block? The health group that has advocated for complete streets is working to get more supporters to attend these meetings, so they won't be so dominated by residents who just received an assessment notice. And with advice from local planners, the engineering staff in charge of the public meetings changed the format so residents would engage directly with one another, giving supporters more of a chance to speak up. More importantly, the assessment system has also been changed so that assessment rates are set—they won't vary based on individual street design elements. Progress is still slow, but some projects have been approved, and the complete streets working group is committed to continuing the education process.

Engaging Leadership

Elected officials, top department officials, and other community leaders are pivotal in the initial adoption of a policy. They are also invaluable during implementation for their ability to encourage continued citizen support, make necessary policy adjustments, and help different agencies within government work together more effectively. They need the professional staff to help them understand their most effective points of intervention and to provide them with good information.

Leaders are important assets in communicating to the public about the changes under way. In Fairhope, Alabama, residents complained about new bike lanes, sharrows, and other features installed to make space for bicycles on the roadway. Their mayor, Tim Kant, responded by acknowledging their concerns but asserting that complete streets are important for safety: "I know the new markings and lines look odd. They are different from what we are used to seeing, and they represent a new way to think about streets and traffic. Streets used to be designed just for the benefit of cars and drivers. New ways of thinking leads to streets that work for everyone and this requires slower traffic."[11] Big-city mayors, from Nashville's Karl Dean to New York mayor Michael Bloomberg, have been prominent champions, working closely with their staffs to consistently communicate with the public about their ongoing support for the changes that are taking place on their streets. Chicago transportation commissioner Gabe Klein says that mayor Rahm Emanuel uses economic arguments to make the case for the innovative projects his agency is putting on Chicago's streets. "What I love about what he does is that he sells it," says Klein. "He sells it based on dollars and cents, and that's something people can't really argue with, no matter where they fall on the political spectrum."

Elected officials can also help practitioners as they are working to untangle that web of automobile-oriented policies discussed in chapter 4. In Arlington County, Virginia, across the Potomac from Washington, DC, members of the county board have found that redirecting transportation policy is an iterative process that benefits from input from the public and leadership. The County has been committed to multimodal transportation for many years, and over time the board has put in place professional staff that shares their views. The Arlington County board also set up bicycle, pedestrian, and transit advisory committees to give input as policies are implemented. County board member Chris Zimmerman says these committees are especially helpful when the agency employees tend to view implementation as a technical issue. "A lot of this is art, not just science," he says. "If the organization doesn't have a way to gauge that and get more input, it may not be able to make decisions that are sustainable."

Advisory boards can help ensure that implementation stays on track. Even so, Zimmerman says the board is constantly called upon to make policy adjustments. He gives the example of Arlington's early traffic calming policies and the need a few years later to rein in the placement of speed humps. He says that the first challenge for board members in making such adjustments is figuring out the policy basis of the problem, when the staff may present all the constraints in the situation as immutable: "The policy makers may not realize that part of what they are getting back [from staff] are not technical, physical or scientific constraints, but are policy items over which the professional has no discretion, but the policy maker does." Staff members can make the process easier if they help identify which constraints are policy related and whether the problem lies at the local, state, or federal level. Then the elected officials can either directly change the policy or work with the state legislature or Congress to get it changed.

One of the most important roles of leaders is in understanding the extent to which bureaucratic silos prevent change, and the role they can play in bringing different departments together to solve common problems. In Philadelphia, deputy mayor Rina Cutler attributes her ability to launch innovative multimodal projects in part to mayor Michael Nutter's reorganization of the city departments.[12] She oversees both transportation and public works, eliminating one of the most troublesome divides; Charlotte's department of transportation is also organized this way.

Jerry Fried, the former mayor of Montclair, New Jersey, is a good example of the role an elected official can play in the Complete Streets movement. He also shares some insight into what support elected officials need in order to engage on this issue. Fried got into politics through bicycle advocacy, but he says that for most residents in this small suburban town north of Newark, that was a negative. Cyclists were viewed as "just a bunch of guys in spandex who want to ride bikes." Complete streets—and being mayor—gave him a platform for going around his community to talk about street design issues with an array of people engaged in civic life. He can rattle them off—the planners, the school district, local business improvement districts, health care providers, the advocacy groups, the YMCA, AARP, the senior citizen advisory committee, the public transportation advisory committee, and more. He notes: "Of course, they are also voters. These are groups that any elected official would want to talk to, particularly around election time; these are the cultural organizations that are the strength of a community. That's one thing I find most inspiring, the shared connections all these groups find around complete streets."

After leaving his post, Fried traveled the state to tell other mayors and council members about the civic connections possible with complete streets. Under the NJDOT-sponsored program Ambassadors in Motion, he provided technical assistance to communities adopting complete streets policies, and he spent more time getting his peers to think about who could they could reach out to in their own communities.

Fried's experience shows that elected officials are most effective when they have a clear vision to share, constituencies they can engage, and a

The transformation of South Park Street in Montclair, New Jersey, had big economic benefits; see chapter 7 for details. (Photos by Arterial, LLC.)

way to talk about the value of complete streets. They are more likely to become champions if they get positive feedback—and if they understand that projects that build better streets can be quick, visible, and popular. The ability to tie the project to benefits from pedestrian safety to long-term economic health makes them even more attractive, especially in relation to other, longer-term problems faced by cities and states.

Complete streets proponents within agencies can seek out and support elected officials to play a pivotal role in creating change. Nurturing even a single council member can help create a valuable ally if the implementation process sparks NIMBY opposition or requires a policy adjustment.

In Boston, policy and planning director Vineet Gupta says Mayor Menino wanted to push bicycling, so when the timing was right proponents introduced him to the broader complete streets concept and the idea of changing the streets by rewriting the design manual. Gupta says, "You need to figure out who in the principal agencies will be champions behind the cause so they can stand up behind you, and you have to get to the people who the mayor trusts. Every chief executive bounces off ideas among close aides. We pushed in all those ways to make sure this was a good fit in the first place." Menino's commitment grew to the point that he was willing to spend political capital on removing parking to make room for parklets, bike lanes, and public transportation.

Complete streets proponents, particularly those who come out of a field where they focused on technical training, may find they need to broaden their interest and raise their personal profiles in order to interact effectively with leadership and make lasting change. In Nashville, Adetokunbo "Toks" Omishakin, a tall, confident Nigerian-American with a master's in planning, was serving as the first bicycle/pedestrian coordinator in the city at the planning department. When he first suggested to some of his colleagues that the city should adopt a complete streets policy, they objected, calling it an unfunded mandate. Omishakin says, "I realized that in order to make a difference I needed to step up and make some personal changes if I wanted to make an impact as the messenger on the issue in the city. At the planning department, I'd reached a ceiling."

When mayor Karl Dean came into office in 2007, he had a strong interest in quality-of-life issues and health—and improving health through active living. Close to two thirds of adults in the region were overweight or obese,[13] and in addition to its low ranking in several national measures of health, the Nashville region has ranked high in measures of sprawl, including a 2010 report that found that among residents of large cities, Nashville commuters spend the most time driving in rush hour.[14] Mayor

Dean established a Bicycle Pedestrian Advisory Committee and tapped
Omishakin to lead it. The position was moved from the planning department into the mayor's office, and Omishakin understood that he could
use the higher profile to expand the scope of the position to reach a wider
circle than was possible when advocating narrowly for bicycling and walking. A new federal program soon gave him the opportunity to connect his
work even more closely to the mayor's interest in the built environment,
transportation, and healthy living. The Communities Putting Prevention to Work program of the Centers for Disease Control and Prevention would focus on policy changes to improve health and would provide $7.5 million to the city. Omishakin wrote components of the grant
and worked to take on leadership of the program from his position in
the mayor's office, and he was named the first director of healthy living
initiatives in Nashville.

Omishakin focused on building a coalition to support policy changes
to encourage physical activity and healthy eating. He made additional recommendations for adoption of a complete streets policy to the mayor,
but Dean didn't agree immediately. He wanted to work through some of
the questions that were raised by opponents. Recalls Omishakin, "The
tipping point was the choir. So many community interests were coming
to the mayor that they overwhelmed his doubts. He came to me one day
and said, 'Toks, we're doing this!'" The mayor's decision came about a
week after a positive editorial in the paper in September 2010. The executive order was signed on Walk to School Day in 2010. This was shortly
after the city council approved a transportation capital spending plan that
directed 62 percent of its funds to multimodal accommodation, helping
ensure the executive order would become a reality on the ground.

Omishakin eventually left Nashville to take on a leadership position
at Tennessee DOT, and he noted the big change he has undergone in his
career: "Often times to make a broad-based impact, people need to get beyond the very technical role they may have played. I went from planning
and designing facilities on the ground, to advancing policy, to having an
influencer position." He notes the transition wasn't about personal ambi-
tion but in part about building influence in order to realize the vision for
complete streets in the city.

Engaging Colleagues

Omishakin says that during his early work building support in Nashville, he did one thing wrong: "I was leaving out one of the main groups of people who would likely be against this idea. In Nashville, some of the pushback was from city engineers. And even a great mayor like Karl Dean needs public works to pave roads, and to build or maintain infrastructure in key districts of the city. He wasn't going to come down on them. So when he heard the public works leadership say this might be an unfunded mandate, he listened." The policy moved forward when all the other voices tipped the balance, but the support of the public works department was still essential to success in implementation. He says, "Our city engineers made great strides prior to the policy adoption and even more afterwards, but it's a hard conversation to have, because you're saying 'Use the limited money you have, and add more things to do with it.'" As discussed in chapter 5, Omishakin's persistence paid off.

In New Jersey, bicycle and pedestrian coordinator Sheree Davis, secure in the support of Commissioner James Simpson, proceeded to meet with the next level of leadership: every assistant commissioner in every department that the policy would affect. She was building relationships at the same time that she was coming to a greater understanding of the process.

Practitioners—engineers *and* planners—also face the need to learn new skills and to approach projects in a fundamentally different way. They have years of education, habits, and strong opinions about how roads should be built, mostly oriented around planning for automobiles. And they need to "own" the concept of complete streets at a deeper level than either the public or elected officials. Winning them over requires much more than formal training.

The first step is addressing their fears that new practices will make them fail in two core missions: improving safety and easing traffic congestion. Most immediately, they worry that unsafe streets will lead to crashes and lawsuits, and that congested roads will lead to complaining citizens, unhappy politicians, and a demand for an explanation. Gary Toth, an engineer who worked for change at New Jersey DOT prior to the Complete Streets movement and who now works for innovative transformation of streets into public spaces, says liability concerns are a bit of a red herring. He and others argue they can be addressed with clear documentation and a better understanding of the risks.[15]

John LaPlante also has impeccable engineering credentials, and one of his favorite themes is debunking the oft-cited statistics about how much congestion costs the economy.[16] He pulls up a slide that walks through the math: if a new design to make a street more pedestrian friendly reduces the speed on a five-mile segment of roadway from forty-five mph to thirty mph, it will take an extra three and one third minutes to go those five miles. Multiply that out by the average daily traffic on the roadway—30,000—and assume all the drivers make $20 an hour for 365 days a year, and those three and one-third minutes add up to $12.1 million a year lost to congestion. This is a simplified version of a calculation taught in engineering schools. It is also used in annual congestions rankings, rolled out each year and repeated by politicians and transportation agencies as part of a plea for more funding for more road capacity. LaPlante will have none of it. When he gets to this point in his presentation, he likes to shock his audience. "Bullsh—t! It is still three and a third minutes, less than the time it takes that person to stop at Starbucks," he says. "Twelve million is a bogus number."

Toth and LaPlante have both traveled the country speaking on these issues, and outside experts can be in the best position to help make a direct challenge to what was seen as conventional wisdom—especially if they can speak to their audience as peers. On a higher level, concerns around the potential for liability and increased traffic congestion are eased and even eliminated when practitioners, especially government employees, understand that the political leadership will back them up. They won't be left to defend these practices on their own: they are backed by a formal complete streets policy, by the statements of their supervisors and elected officials, and by community groups actively supporting the changes. Understanding this base of support takes time and requires exposure to the inclusive decision-making processes outlined in chapter 4.

A champion who understands the challenge of bringing practitioners along is Scott Bradley, an optimistic landscape architect who has been overseeing the complete streets implementation process inside the Minnesota DOT. Once he has addressed the fears of department employees, he doesn't get all vague and visionary—he turns to their day-to-day concerns. He remembers when "the light went on" for a reluctant engineer at a roundtable discussion in Northfield, Minnesota, fifty miles south of the Twin Cities: "He's thinking, [this guy] will be talking about sustainability.' But when I started talking about maintenance and operation concerns, this engineer busted in and said, 'That's it! We need to figure this stuff out! This is wonderful stuff, but how do we find the resources, how do we make it work, how do we get snow and ice off the roads in time for the bicyclists and pedestrians we are expecting, how do we deal with adjacent landowners?'" Bradley says the key is to be able to use success stories in getting practitioners involved in more constructive discussions that help them systematically work through challenges. "Room for innovative problem solving gets 'em talking," he says. "It helps if they see there is some hope and some resources, and somebody from MNDOT to help them."

Fortunately, MNDOT has success stories to tell to engineers across the state, from its years of work on context-sensitive solutions projects, which adapt highway projects to fit the surrounding environment and often include multimodal elements. "[The engineers] are thinking, 'this thing is probably a death trap,' but then they hear that crashes have been reduced by more than 50-60-70 percent, and that it costs less money than traditional solutions, and it has less adverse impact on businesses or the environment, and folks are happy with it," says Bradley, who is director of context sensitive solutions (CSS). "It is those kinds of stories they need to hear."

Another advantage for MNDOT is that their leadership in context-sensitive solutions work has given them an easy way to see complete streets as a continuation of a direction they were already going—rather than a repudiation of past practice. Pushed by advocates in the Minnesota Complete Streets Coalition, and by local governments adopting policies, then–state DOT commissioner Tom Sorel acknowledged the culture change that would need to happen inside the agency. His selection of the CSS division to spearhead it signaled the high priority he placed on seeing through the changes.

The most important thing to remember when working with practitioners, and particularly engineers, is that they are problem solvers. Once they have grasped the problem, they can be set loose on generating solutions. In Wichita, Kansas, the chief engineer was skeptical of complete streets and grudgingly agreed to drop by a "Better Blocks" installation—in which volunteers spend a weekend transforming an unremarkable street into a walkable, bikeable place, with temporary bike lanes, parklets, pedestrian bulb-outs, and many other features.[17] The engineer, who had said he'd come for a few minutes, stayed for three hours. He moved around planters, watched their impact on car speeds, and was totally absorbed in solving the problem of creating a safe street for all users. Wichita may never be the same.

Charlotte Sells Transformation—One Project at a Time

Complete streets proponents are called upon to use all of their persuasive power when a project comes along that starts to reallocate road space. One of the first and most challenging large projects undertaken in Charlotte, North Carolina, was the conversion of East Boulevard, a busy (20,000 average daily traffic) four-lane, undivided roadway with many business uses and high pedestrian and bicycle traffic. The roadway had automobile speeds well in excess of the posted speed limit, too few designated pedestrian crossings, and a significant number of nonmotorized crashes. To create a safer, more inviting environment in line with residents' interests, the city planned a road conversion, with several new pedestrian crossings and carefully designed pedestrian refuge islands. Research shows that these changes reduce speed and conflicts, as fast-moving cars can no longer slalom through traffic and left-turning vehicles have clearer sight-lines. Bicycles and pedestrians have a safer place to travel.

The challenge in converting this roadway was in convincing a skeptical public that fewer automobile lanes wouldn't result in perpetual backups. The local paper ran a disparaging editorial cartoon when the idea was first raised, before the complete streets policy had been formally adopted. During and immediately after construction, residents expressed dismay in public forums at the unfamiliar design; the term *road diet* wasn't going over well on what was known as a busy roadway.

Yet, the project proceeded because of consistent support from the city's leadership and careful outreach by the transportation department staff that brought many residents on board. The staff, led by planning and design division manager Norm Steinman, included Dan Gallagher, Tracy Newsome, and several other professionals with a strong and clear commitment to the new approach. The staff made sure the neighborhood was informed about how the "diet" would work, and about its safety benefits, and they encouraged residents and businesses to express their support to city council. Steinman and his colleagues were also careful to document the project's success. Once the conversion was completed, they compared "before" and "after" measurements to confirm that the changes reduced speeds and traffic crashes. Positive comments about the conversion began to surface from citizens and the media, and particularly from the bicycle community, which praised the project. One lesson: in subsequent projects, they switched to the term *road conversion*.

The process has become easier as citizens have been able to see that changes, including conversions, worked to create streets that worked for cars *and* for other users. And the department has kept up constant

A road conversion and an improved crossing give neighborhood children
in Charlotte better access to a school (at right in photo).
(Photos courtesy Mecklenburg County and Pictometry International.)

communication with the public about the changed philosophy. Steinman says, "The central argument has to be, do you believe that people should be able to walk, to ride bicycles, to get to transit, or do you believe that people should only have to drive everywhere? Once you get past that yes or no part then everything goes nicely, because then you can say, 'if you want people to walk, do you want them to walk in the travel lane? That's not very good, that's not very safe.'" Charlotte has transformed miles of streets and intersections, guided by this this simple belief in safety.

An inexpensive crosswalk helped complete Adams Avenue in San Diego.
(Photo courtesy Alec Hamilton/Walk San Diego.)

CHAPTER SEVEN

Answering a Loaded Question: How Much Do Complete Streets Cost?

I N 2000, SEVENTEEN-YEAR-OLD Nate Oglesby was hit by a car and killed while riding his bicycle home from his job at a Jewel-Osco grocery store in Cary, Illinois. He had to use US 14 to cross the Fox River, but the state highway bridge had been built in the early 1990s without a sidewalk or bike path. He rode in the median—the only place he could find to ride.

What happened next is a lesson in the cost of incomplete streets. His family sued, mainly to find out exactly what happened to Nate; the investigation confirmed he did nothing wrong. The state settled the lawsuit for $80,000. His mother and the community pushed hard to retrofit the bridge with a side path, urging Illinois DOT to act while also launching a grassroots effort to raise money locally. The village of Fox River Grove and Cary and Algonquin Townships together paid about 30 percent of the more than $700,000 price tag of hanging a structure to carry a side path alongside the bridge. Fox River Grove set a paver in the path, naming it "Nate's Crossing."

The story helped get a complete streets law passed in Illinois, and the National Complete Streets Coalition usually tells it to point out how much the Illinois DOT could have saved by providing this side path in the original bridge construction rather than retrofitting it later. But it has another message: how much value a community places on safe travel for its residents. In this case, quite a lot.

The citizens of Cary, Illinois, were clear about the value of pulling the money together to create Nate's Crossing. But they had an obvious (if expensive) project, and a clear need. How can jurisdictions determine how much it will cost to complete their entire transportation network for all users, or even how much the commitment may affect next year's transportation budget? This question usually pops up as a prime concern among agencies that are starting to move toward a complete streets approach. Most problematic, the question seems to ask for an objective dollar figure, but it is loaded with assumptions that proponents must address. Because of those assumptions, it turns out this question has four answers, each addressed in this chapter; each will satisfy different audiences.[1]

Where to Start

Unfortunately, the first impulse of many complete streets advocates is to give an answer to the costs question that does not provide what most transportation professionals are looking for. The professionals see trouble: they are assuming this will cost a lot, they know they have a limited budget, and they are wondering if this is worth it. The advocates zero in on the last point, because of course this is a question of values. But they do so by pointing to the values that *they* think are most important: they tell practitioners that, eventually, complete streets will reduce spending on health care costs, or will add economic value to neighborhoods, or will make the community more sustainable or livable.

These arguments can be compelling to other advocates and to some elected officials and are often essential during the policy-adoption process. The trouble is, when it comes to implementation, these benefits do nothing to help a public works administrator figure out how to balance his or her transportation budget. All of these broader societal savings won't show up on that bottom line, so they are not likely to be convincing. Such arguments still avoid the practical question of how to pay for the change, and they don't address the (incorrect) assumption that this will be expensive. And depending on just how skeptical the planners or engineers are, discussing sustainability may or may not win converts. This is why this "lasting value" answer should be the last one to turn to when discussing complete streets with someone concerned about the practical side of paying for them.

We Have an Urgent Safety Problem

A better starting point to the cost question is the answer that carried the day in Cary, Illinois: that existing users of the street need to be safe. Remember the poll of practitioners in Oklahoma and Texas who were doubtful of the value of complete streets? Their responses assumed that nonmotorized transportation was optional and that no one did or would want to use the street without a car. With that mind-set, the cost of providing these "amenities" is seen as an option—a luxury that strapped transportation departments can ill afford. As discussed in chapter 3, safety is already the best way to motivate practitioners. Changing the framing of the cost question to an immediate safety issue changes the entire equation. How can a transportation department claim that it can't afford to build safer streets, when safety is its core mission?

So, the first fact to establish in making this argument is that people are already using the streets via foot, bicycle, and public transportation. We know that in the one hundred largest cities in the United States, 7.5 million households don't have access to a car.[2] "Goat trails" offer hard visual evidence that people are walking in these "unwalkable" places, as do photographs of people walking, bicycling, or waiting for a bus in those same places.[3] Statistics about travel patterns help—the more local, the better. In New Orleans, complete streets supporters pointed to census data showing that 10.3 percent of residents do not have access to a car and that 8.4 percent walk, bike, or take transit to work in the metro New Orleans area. This can be an effective point to make to transportation professionals who view safe travel as fundamental to their jobs and to elected officials who feel a sense of responsibility for ensuring that taxpayer investments provide for their constituents' needs.

The need to protect existing users is a helpful point to make when someone says transportation funds should be reserved for building facilities to serve cars because the money comes from gas taxes paid by drivers. Those who use the roads without buying gasoline are still helping to pay for them through income taxes, sales taxes, property taxes, bonds, and fees. A report from the U.S. Public Interest Research Group shows that, contrary to popular belief, roads do not pay for themselves: today, only half the cost of road construction and maintenance is covered by funds

A "goat track" on Route 1 in northern Virginia is evidence that people
walk along this road. (Photo by Barbara McCann.)

from gasoline taxes. Since World War II, road construction costs have out-
paced funds raised through the gas tax and other road-user fees by $600
billion—money that came out of general government funds.[4]

This Won't Break the Bank

But even with a compelling case for meeting the needs of people now
using the roads, the fact remains that transportation funding is tight. At
both the federal and state levels, it is difficult to gather the political support needed to raise the gas tax or to find new sources for replacing this
dwindling source of revenue. How can transportation agencies take on
what looks to be an enormous additional expense in times like these?

In Richfield, Minnesota, a utility project led to the reconfiguration of 76th Street (top left) with sidewalks, a side path, and fewer lanes. Residents to the east (top right) want the same. (Aerial courtesy Google Earth; photo by Steve Elkins.)

Decision makers need to be reassured that complete streets can be achieved within existing transportation budgets or, in other words, that "this won't break the bank." This answer to the costs question corrects several common misconceptions about what the term *complete streets* really means. Every complete street project won't be a multimodal boulevard with all the pedestrian bulb-out bells and landscaped-median whistles, and practitioners need to hear this. Many improvements are modest in size and low in cost. At first, complete streets can mean nothing more than a widened shoulder. For example, while San Diego has gotten a lot of attention for the dramatic conversion of La Jolla Boulevard (discussed in chapter 2), the region's commitment to safety for everyone has also led to many far more modest improvements. The city added a midblock crossing to Adams Avenue so residents of the University Heights neighborhood could reach Trolley Barn Park. It cost only $20,000, but it provided residents in a lower-income neighborhood with safe access to their only park.[5] Another low-cost solution came in at just $4,500; it used paint and a few bollards to slow traffic at the 50th and University Avenue intersection (this example can be seen in the image that opens this chapter).

An important strategy for efficient implementation is to look for opportunities to make changes as part of existing projects, particularly maintenance and repair projects, as discussed in chapter 5—for example, most of the Salt Lake City bike lane expansion was achieved with existing maintenance funds.

Infrastructure repair projects also present an opportunity. In Richfield, Minnesota, a Twin Cities suburb located in Hennepin County, the city expected to use $6 million in street reconstruction bonds to replace a sewer line and reconstruct 76th Street above it. The consulting engineer worked with members of the community; they wanted the project to also reduce highway overflow traffic and help complete a trail linkage. The project ended up converting the four-lane roadway to two lanes with sidewalks, plantings, and a separated side path. The new configuration cost $2 million less to build. It looks strikingly different from the old—and is so popular that residents on an adjoining section of 76th are now demanding the same.

Thinking Ahead Saves Money

The previous example shows that thinking ahead can save money. The same discovery has been made from Washington State to Florida. In Washington State, the department of transportation determined that using a complete streets process would have reduced the schedule, scope, and budget changes that are common to improvement projects on highways serving as small-town Main Streets. The study found that this planning ahead could save an average of $9 million per project, or about 30 percent.[6] A pilot project incorporated early community input and added sidewalks, safe crossings, on-street parking, and other features important to small towns; the new costs were offset by the reduction in unexpected changes. In Lee County Florida, the county staff reexamined the list of road projects approved in the Long Range Transportation Plan in light of their new complete streets policy. They determined that five roads slated for widening from two to four lanes could instead be fitted with turn lanes and medians, creating a safer environment with minimal impact on traffic. They estimate the changes will reduce the cost of these five projects by $58.5 million, a significant savings for the county and its taxpayers that will also create streets that are better for all users.

Practitioners are reassured to know that complete streets implementation does not require simply tacking on additional space for a bike lane or a sidewalk to every street project. They may assume that when space is tight, the only option is to widen the street—and to them that brings up the specter of right-of-way acquisition, which is both expensive and time consuming. Lee County's discovery of road conversions is just one example of a flexible approach to design that focuses on a creative allocation of existing space.

During policy adoption, many jurisdictions also set limits on how far a project must go to accommodate all users. Such limits are a reasonable part of the conversation, but setting strict percentages, such as 5 or 20 percent of a total project budget, also limits judgment calls.[7] For example, on a highly used corridor with dangerous attributes and a challenging geometry, higher spending levels may be necessary to achieve safety goals. Over time, the new approach will change the decision-making process itself, so it will become increasingly difficult to identify what expenditures can be attributed directly to the complete streets policy.

Costs Are Not Fixed

For years, the Charlotte department of transportation sidestepped questions about the cost of creating complete streets. Planning and design division manager Norm Steinman believed that providing a number would just allow people from each side to use the number for their own ends.

Steinman says, "It is relatively easy to estimate cost. You can find information if you look hard enough, to calculate correctly the incremental costs.
What is impossible is to calculate the value. What is the value to people
of having a sidewalk?" He thinks intangible values, such as safety and how
residents feel about their neighborhoods, are far more important.

He also felt that questions about costs held an inaccurate underlying
assumption: that costs are fixed in the first place. The most accurate answer to the question "How much does a mile of sidewalk cost?" is "It depends." Does it cross any streams? Does right-of-way need to be acquired?
What is the current cost of asphalt, concrete, or labor?

In Charlotte, Steinman demonstrated this variability with an analysis
of NCDOT projects. His staff analyzed the line item bid costs for 135 final
construction contracts let by NCDOT over several years. Each year, con-
tract costs, which include planning, design, mobilizing resources, grading,
erosion control, traffic control, and curb and gutter, varied by as much
as 18 percent above or 12 percent below a baseline set in 2010.[8] Most of
that variability was due to changing economic conditions and the fluctu-
ating price of crude oil—the base ingredient for asphalt. Looking more
closely at three projects, they determined that bicycle lanes added about
5 percent to planning, design, and construction costs (not including right-
of-way acquisition); sidewalks, about 3 percent. Narrowing lanes from the
twelve-foot standard to eleven feet, on the other hand, reduced construction costs by about 2 percent. The point was not to pin down the costs
of "adding on" bicycle and pedestrian infrastructure—it was to show that
the costs of these clearly beneficial features were so minor as to dwindle
to near insignificance in the face of the annual variations that NCDOT
had come to expect and accept in other budget line items.

The annual variability may help explain why early cost concerns often
seem to evaporate once implementation is in full swing. In the early days
of the National Complete Streets Coalition, we searched for cities and
states that could estimate the impact on their budgets due to changing to
complete streets practices; not only were we unable to find any, but those
early adopters seemed pretty unconcerned with pinning down a figure.
Creating a safe environment for all users had become just one part of
a much bigger calculation—and one with unquestioned value. Projects
simply became part of the existing transportation budget.

The reassurance provided by this answer is most effective when doubters know that a nearby jurisdiction has adopted a complete streets approach without instigating a budgetary crisis. This understanding rarely comes by looking at a bottom-line figure or a spreadsheet—it arrives with stories told, places visited, and one-on-one conversations between peers.

Complete Streets Can Unlock New Financial Resources

If the second answer to the question of how much complete streets cost delivers reassurance, the third answer instills hope. Multimodal projects can make transportation investments more popular with citizens and elected officials and can garner more support for transportation funding—and the new commitment can help unlock new resources.

The paving crew in Arlington County, Virginia, that encountered a cheering family while installing a bike lane won't soon forget that show of support. In Arlington and elsewhere, this support translates into dollars. Arlington levies a commercial property tax devoted to transportation purposes, and between 2009 and 2011 about one third of it ($19 million) went to complete street improvements and almost $35 million to public transportation.[9] The voters have also approved bonds to pay for specific projects. In Seattle, voters approved the $365 million "Bridging the Gap" levy in part because of its promise to improve the transit, bicycle, pedestrian, and motorist networks. The city had done polling to gauge support for the measure, and according to former bicycle-pedestrian coordinator Peter Lagerwey, "We just kept adding in bicycle, pedestrian, and transit improvements until it reached the threshold where it would pass." In Nashville, strong community support allowed mayor Karl Dean to set aside $12.5 million for sidewalks, $3 million for bikeways, and more than $10 million for public transportation in his 2010–2011 budget.

Generalized support can also be expressed in terms of dollars and cents. When given a dollar to divide according to the portion that should go to different modes of transportation, Minnesota poll respondents allocated 20 cents to bicycling and walking facilities, 25 cents to public transportation, and 55 cents to roads for cars. That 2008 poll helped drive the state to adopt its complete streets policy, which is now being implemented across the state.

These examples show how community transportation priorities are changing, and funding will change with it. Agencies that are accustomed to securing funding through a drumbeat of promised congestion relief may take a while to understand that other outcomes can also garner support—and in fact may be the key to their future.

A complete streets approach can open the door to new funding opportunities. In Montclair, New Jersey, former mayor Jerry Fried says his town's commitment to a new approach helped it secure funds from a variety of sources, ranging from federal Safe Routes to School funding to a state planning grant to pilot program funding. Now, many New Jersey towns have a financial incentive for adopting complete streets policies: the highly competitive NJDOT Local Aid grant program gives towns an extra point in the review process if they have a policy. MPOs, such as those serving Kansas City, Nashville, and Columbus, are also establishing systems that give an edge to multimodal policies and projects.

The US Department of Transportation's TIGER (Transportation Investment Generating Economic Recovery) program put a premium on multimodal projects, and places with complete streets policies have received many of the grants. Dubuque, Iowa, received one of the first TIGER grants; the city has received national media attention for its innovative reworking of a network of streets in the historic Millwork district, using $5.6 million in TIGER funds and a $150,000 Iowa Great Places grant. With a policy in place since early 2011, Birmingham, Alabama, won $10 million from the very competitive program in a later round. The money will be invested in safer streets for all users in the downtown Civil Rights district; in rebuilding streets in a tornado-ravaged neighborhood to better serve all travelers; and in creating better connection for the off-road trail system. New Haven, Connecticut, home to a strong complete streets policy and process, received a $16 million TIGER grant to turn a grade-separated highway into a signature multimodal boulevard. Note that these projects did not fund a narrow set of nonmotorized facilities but added value for all users of the transportation network.

The process of establishing the need for safe access for everyone in a community can inspire a search for new sources of funds. The process of developing a complete streets policy in the small community of Pipestone, Minnesota, drummed up interest in the state Safe Routes to School program and led to a successful funding application.

US transportation secretary Ray LaHood celebrates a new complete streets district in Dubuque, Iowa on May 18, 2012. (Photo courtesy City of Dubuque.)

One caution in pointing toward new funding sources: if this comes up before decision makers have a full understanding of the commitment they are being asked to make, they may fall back into the habit of thinking in silos and assume that making any changes depends on new, separate funding sources. Topeka, Kansas, started out this way, passing a policy but making its implementation contingent on a special complete streets fund. Specific funding allocations, such as the 1 percent set-asides in Oregon and Connecticut, may also result in one-dimensional spending plans that do little to change agency practices or priorities. The complete streets approach, by definition, means using existing transportation funds in a new way, to ensure the safety of everyone on the street.

The inclusive decision-making process that takes hold under the complete streets approach can lead to new funding solutions closer to home, as the breaking down of funding silos helps practitioners think of the "transportation budget" in the broadest possible terms. Colorado Springs has created much of its bicycle network by thinking ahead and using maintenance funds, but transportation planner Kristin Bennett cautions, "If you're going to afford this, you have to stop worrying about, 'my [funding] pot is over here, and your pot is over there.'" For example, by working with a community development specialist, she found $850 million in community development block grant program money to help make improvements to regional trails.

Transit agencies are often strapped and have less secure funding streams than roadways; their leaders are usually reluctant to push for street improvements because they may be asked to pay for them. The Louisville, Kentucky, transit agency, TARC, is an exception. Director Barry Barker put $800,000 of his agency's money on the table in a bid to partner with the city and county to invest a million dollars in improving street access to bus stops. Once the city and county merged and moved toward complete streets, the transit agency and the planning and public works departments began to collaborate in earnest, working together to find the most economical way to make improvements.

For transit agencies, this can become a money-saving approach because of the high cost of paratransit service. Some people with disabilities use paratransit service because their neighborhoods lack the sidewalks and curb cuts they would need to reach regular bus service. The Maryland Transit Administration found that providing paratransit for a daily commuter costs far more—$38,500 a year—than adding basic improvements to transit stops.[10]

In Boston, the careful development of the new *Complete Streets Manual* also led to a new discussion of who pays for what, especially when it comes to maintaining new infrastructure. The manual establishes three categories of treatments: standard, enhanced, and pilot. The city will maintain standard treatments, but if a developer or neighborhood wants enhanced features, such as special brick pavers, they may have to sign a maintenance agreement. While the policy has drawbacks, especially for neighborhoods that can't afford special treatments, it draws more players into responsibility for creating quality streets.

Finally, many cities and states are financing ambitious transportation projects by capturing a portion of the increased property values and sales taxes a project is expected to bring. The most common method for this is tax increment financing, which designates a district and dedicates a portion of the expected increase in tax revenue in that district to paying off the debt incurred in building a project.

Investing in Complete Streets Will Add Lasting Value

After offering reassurance and hope, complete streets proponents can inspire by making the case for the tremendous value represented by an investment in multimodal streets. These values come through lives saved, healthier citizens, stronger local economies with more sustainable practices, and even through less traffic congestion. When addressing the issue of costs, these benefits should be presented in fiscal terms. All of the examples below attach a dollar figure to benefits that are sometimes hard to quantify.

Again, safety is the first and best way to answer the costs question, and it can be translated into dollars and cents. The national pedestrian safety study *Dangerous by Design* cited National Safety Council estimates that each pedestrian fatality cost $4.3 million.[11] In a presentation to colleagues, New Jersey's Sharee Davis used the figure to justify NJDOT's investment, noting that the 1,514 pedestrian deaths cost the state $6.51 billion over ten years.

The public health community has assembled an impressive array of studies and statistics that document the costs of physical inactivity, some of which can be attributed to a hostile street environment.[12] Nationally, health expenses related to obesity are estimated to range from $147 billion to nearly $210 billion per year.[13] A California study found that overweight, obese, and sedentary residents cost San Diego County more than $3 billion a year in health care expenses and lost productivity.[14] We know that changing the built environment helps solve this problem: one study surveyed residents in eleven countries and found that those who lived in neighborhoods with sidewalks on most streets were 47 percent more likely to reach the minimum level of physical activity for health, and that those in neighborhoods with bike lanes and bus stops were even more active.[15]

Studies have found that facilities that encourage walking and bicycling deliver quantifiable health benefits far in excess of their construction or maintenance costs. One study launched as part of a complete streets initiative in the Birmingham, Alabama, region projected the costs and benefits of dramatically expanding bus service in the suburb of Fairfax, including the addition of stops, shelters, and sidewalks. They calculated the fiscal impact of air quality improvements, better access to medical facilities, reductions in traffic crashes, savings in personal vehicle costs, and savings related to traffic reduction. The authors found that over twelve years, each dollar invested in building and operating the new system and its sidewalks would generate $2.05 in return.[16]

Many of the cities profiled in this book have invested in complete streets as part of a broader initiative to rein in health care costs by getting residents on their feet. In Nashville, the region's health care industry and public health officials have made a strong fiscal argument for investing in multimodal transportation.[17] The director of public health testified in support of the Major and Collector Street Plan, and getting someone outside of the transportation planning world to step up in support of the investment made a big difference in its acceptance. From Los Angeles to Bloomington, Indiana, to Boston, the health argument has helped support a different set of transportation investments.

Some communities are including complete streets as part of their far-reaching plans to reduce carbon emissions. Portland, Oregon, has done the most to track its progress, noting that transportation emissions have dropped below 1990 levels and that per-person emissions have fallen 22 percent since 1990. By one calculation, Portlanders have saved $1.1 billion annually by driving less than other Americans; put another way, the carbon savings from driving less are worth between $28 and $70 million annually.[18]

The economic value of good health or reducing carbon pollution applies across the population over time and is quite difficult to pin down. But when the goal is economic growth, the case can sometimes be made that specific projects will end up paying for themselves. This is especially compelling for elected officials. In Montclair, New Jersey, the rehabilitation of South Park Street was intended to transform it from a "dangerous obstacle to walking" into a street worthy of becoming a civic center. The

Facing page: Lancaster, California, transformed its dangerous, busy main street into "the BLVD" to improve safety and bring businesses downtown. It has become a focal point of special events. (Photos: Before by City of Lancaster; aerial by Tamara Leigh Photography; event by Curt Gideon Photography.)

project would widen the sidewalk, add a pedestrian island, plant trees, and much more. The city's capital finance committee found that the project would dramatically increase commercial property values in the central business district. Increased tax revenues over ten years were projected to be double the cost of the project. The results demonstrated the value of placemaking to a small city with a limited commercial tax base. The data helped the city decide to issue bonds to pay for what could have been dismissed as a random beautification project. The head of the Montclair Center Business Improvement District says the renovation sparked commercial interest even before it was completed.

Numerous studies have confirmed that cities can indeed bank on it: complete streets improvements and land use changes increase retail sales and property values along specific corridors and in certain districts.[19] The town of Lancaster in Los Angeles County experienced a big drop in crashes after it transformed its main drag, Lancaster Boulevard. It had been an unpleasant and dangerous high-speed roadway that had kept pedestrians and shoppers away. The award-winning new design, installed in 2010, removed six traffic signals and created a central "Rambla" patterned after the design of a street in Barcelona, Spain, which provides parking spaces, pedestrian facilities, and a place for community events. The $10 million investment in new lighting, landscaping, and trees spurred $125 million in investment in the downtown area, with forty new businesses opening and eight hundred new jobs. Sales tax revenue grew by 26 percent. The project is so popular with residents that the road is now affectionately referred to as "the BLVD."

Economic benefits are also accruing in New York. As crashes drop, retail sales rise. The New York City DOT documented a 49 percent increase in retail sales at locally owned businesses along a stretch of 9th Avenue in Manhattan redesigned for all users. In the Bronx, the DOT made changes to Fordham Street to speed buses, and sales rose 71 percent. Commercial vacancies dropped surrounding the city's new pedestrian plazas.[20]

A recent study from the Brookings Institution found that for Washington, DC, neighborhoods, each step up the rung of a five-step walkability ladder added value to office, retail, and apartment rents, as well as increased home values.[21] Improved transit service also provides economic benefits, and streetcars in particular are being installed to help boost economic development along specific corridors in Los Angeles, Arlington (Virginia), Cincinnati (Ohio), and other cities. As will be discussed in chapter 8, the Cleveland HealthLine Bus Rapid Transit project reallocated street space for the use of high-capacity buses, bicycles, and pedestrians; the line attracted at least $4.3 billion in development along Euclid Avenue before it even opened.[22] For many proponents of smart growth and complete streets, this new model of economic growth is the most compelling long-term answer to how communities will pay for a complete streets transformation.

A commitment to complete streets can provide one more type of lasting value, which gets back to a central concern of many transportation professionals: congestion relief. A few places are pursuing a multimodal strategy to reduce delay without constant capacity expansion. Portland, Oregon, officials are fond of noting that the city's entire bicycle network would cost about $60 million to build all at once, about equivalent to one mile of a four-lane urban freeway, and in 2008 that network provided for the commuting needs of about 6 percent of Portlanders.[23] Completing the streets won't by itself make much of a dent in solving traffic congestion; it is well known that Portland has employed a range of land use and transit strategies. Arlington, Virginia, knows this and regards multimodal street improvements as providing support for an ambitious transportation demand management (TDM) program. In 2011, Arlington County Commuter Services estimated that its program reduced traffic in Arlington by forty-five thousand car trips each workday, by helping people switch from driving to taking transit, carpooling, vanpooling, walking, or bicycling.[24] Transit improvements and multimodal streets provide the base on which the county has built a full-service TDM program that reaches out to businesses, operates retail commuter stores, offers guaranteed rides home, and does much more to help commuters get out of their cars.

Lasting Value Catch-22

Multimodal streets offer other long-term benefits, from improving transit speeds to creating greater social capital through placemaking. I particularly recommend Todd Litman's interesting cost and benefit analysis of complete streets.[25] But the connection between dollars spent on road projects and money saved elsewhere can be hard to calculate. And the places that have succeeded in translating the benefits into dollars have something in common—they are almost all from cities or regions that already hold a strikingly different vision of how their transportation network can best serve their communities. Quantifying this value—through car trips avoided, health costs spared, or businesses opened—requires collecting data and making connections in new ways. Many communities are not yet able to make these connections, so proving these bigger benefits when multimodal investments are first proposed is something of a catch-22.

A solution is at hand: patience. Most places that make the commitment to complete their streets will do so because they have come to believe that ensuring the safety of everyone using the road is "worth it," and they have gained confidence that they won't break the bank. In time, elected officials, agency leaders, and citizens should come to see the potential for much more.

This realization may come easier as officials recognize the tremendous cost of continued lane expansion for cars, especially at a time of decreasing resources. Massachusetts's secretary of transportation Richard Davey bluntly declared in 2012 that his state wouldn't be building any more superhighways, declaring, "There is no room."[26] The Tennessee DOT halted construction of the long-planned I-69, noting it would sap funds needed for repair and safety improvements on the rest of the state's roads. They may be emboldened by new challenges to the conventional wisdom that congestion is economically disastrous; one analysis of the economic growth rates and congestion rankings of US cities found that cities with more delay have a higher gross domestic product.[27]

It is clear that deciding how to pay for complete streets requires a shift in priorities, and many communities are showing the way as they realign their budgets and spending patterns to create safer streets. The next question is exactly *what* to pay for: What will successfully balance the needs of different people vying for use of the roadways for driving, walking, bicycling, or catching the bus?

A protected bike lane in Chicago gives children a place to ride on the street.
(Photo courtesy Chicago DOT.)

CHAPTER EIGHT

The Balancing Act: Setting Priorities for Different Users

M AKING A COMMITMENT TO complete streets breaks open a tidy linear system that has traditionally delivered roads designed only to speed motor vehicles to their destinations. The transportation project pipeline was good at taking in a narrow set of inputs at one end and pouring out a finished road at the other. Agencies must now bring many more modes, voices, and considerations into the process all along the way. What was a pipeline can become something of a swamp; everyone involved may end up feeling caught in a morass of competing claims for limited roadway space and limited funding. Rather than simply delivering a project, transportation professionals must navigate their way toward a solution that may not quite satisfy anyone.

Who Gets Priority?

To help decide this question, agencies are using new systems to translate the complete streets policy commitment into funding decisions and projects on the ground, fashioning charts and scoring systems to help them strike a balance between road users with different and sometimes incompatible needs. But before discussing these systems, it is important to acknowledge that allocating road space won't be a wholly rational process. All the players have something at stake, but they don't all have the same capacity to fight for it.

Drivers

Automobiles have long been in the driver's seat in every aspect of transportation project delivery. And you could say, rightly so; some 83 percent of the trips Americans made in 2009 were made in private automobiles.[1] Automobile-oriented transportation models and Level of Service indicators remain the primary methods of predicting and providing for travel needs. Cars take up a tremendous amount of space on the roadway and require significant storage space as well. But until recently, meeting those spatial demands has simply been part of the transportation professionals' job. This may be why motorists' or truckers' groups are generally not members of complete streets advisory groups; their interests have been assumed to be represented by the transportation professionals.

On a national level, motorists organized decades ago, into the American Highway Users Alliance and the American Automobile Association (AAA). They've worked closely with the construction industry through the American Road and Transportation Builders Association and with state transportation agencies through AASHTO to keep federal transportation funding on track and to keep the road-building pipeline filled with projects. They have worked against including a complete streets provision in the federal transportation bill. Freight haulers are also a major player, as trucks move 70 percent of the nation's goods (by weight).

At the local level, the position of motorists' groups on the shifting streetscape has been mixed. Local AAA representatives have argued both *against* protected bike lanes in Washington, DC, and *for* a new complete streets law in Philadelphia. In a few cases, ad hoc groups of motorists have complained in the media about "a war on cars" or have launched protest websites or petitions, usually against specific projects.

The biggest challenge in serving drivers is that most Americans expect free parking and relatively uncongested roads that are kept that way through road widenings. These goals inevitably get a lower priority when building a walkable, transit- and bicycle-friendly transportation network. Frankly, drivers have the most to lose when priorities start to shift, but in terms of passenger transportation, people who drive can also be people who walk, bicycle, or take transit. And the assumption that all American adults identify as drivers is changing. Young people are delaying getting their licenses, and some younger drivers no longer buy and care for a beloved car but opt instead to borrow one through the successful new car-sharing industry. Frustrated commuters look for other options on weekends, and for more active options for their children. The growing population of older drivers wants slower, safer roads, as well as alternatives to driving. But even as people diversify their personal transportation portfolio, serving drivers will remain of primary importance in much of America, where automobile-oriented land uses will take decades to change.

Pedestrians

At the other end of the scale, pedestrians take up the least space, require the most fine-grained planning, and, oddly, have little direct clout in the transportation planning process. Since everyone is a pedestrian, advocates have had a tough time organizing a stand-alone "pedestrian lobby," but urban thinkers and planners now see walkability as central to achieving the broader goals of economic growth, health, and livability—and they recognize pedestrians' vulnerability in streets filled with cars. So, some cities are reversing decades of practice that put cars first. Gabe Klein, Chicago's transportation commissioner, says, "Our priority has to be the people walking, because they have the least armor."[2]

Putting pedestrians first obviously means more space for sidewalks and higher-quality crosswalks, a relatively easy lift. What is harder is creating the connectivity that pedestrians need. They are the most sensitive to being sent out of their way, and that proves a challenge in suburban areas with dendritic street networks; new pedestrian cut throughs are almost never popular with existing homeowners. Another potential conflict is over allocating more time to pedestrians: a walkable environment is one where people have time to cross the streets and where drivers are moving at slower, safer speeds.

Pedestrians with different needs are starting to get some attention in the planning process; AARP has been a powerful and active proponent of complete streets as part of its push to help the growing number of older Americans age in place. The number of Americans over age sixty-five is expected to more than double by 2025, and they will make up one fifth of the total population. AARP sponsored one of the very first studies of a complete streets approach, *Planning Complete Streets for an Aging America*, which addresses the needs of older drivers as well as older pedestrians, summarizing three basic strategies: design for slower speeds, make navigation easier, and simplify signage.[3] AARP is now creating new resources to help its state- and local-level volunteers work to ensure that complete streets policies result in changes on the ground.

At the other end of the life cycle, parents and public health advocates want to create safe walking routes to schools, so kids can get daily physical activity. The Safe Routes to School (SRTS) movement goes beyond infrastructure changes (which are termed "engineering") to address four other "Es" of the walk to school: educating children about safe walking, encouraging families to value active travel to school, enforcing laws for safe walking, and evaluating the success of SRTS initiatives. Beginning in 2005, the federal Safe Routes to School program provided resources on how best to create safer streets for children and dedicated millions of dollars each year to SRTS grants, but the entire program would cover less than 6 percent of the schools in the United States.[4] The SRTS National Partnership is working in communities across the country for complete streets policies that will help close the gap.

Many people with lower incomes rely on walking, public transportation, and bicycling because they cannot afford to own a car. A few campaigns led by public health advocates have sought to organize these road users to push for change, but more frequently, they are drawn into complete streets planning processes via robust public involvement efforts that target them and their needs (see the section later in this chapter about including equity issues in transportation planning).

People who use wheelchairs and have low vision would seem to have a strong tool to ensure their place on the street through the Americans with Disabilities Act, which is enforced through the US Justice Department. But the ADA does not require installation of new sidewalks on roads where they don't already exist—that's one reason that so many wheelchair ramps at curb cuts lead to nowhere. The ramp is required as part of pouring the curb, but the sidewalk is not. In addition, for many years, the street standards written for the ADA were inadequate and outdated; much-improved draft regulations have been awaiting final approval since 2005. Some groups of people with disabilities have become engaged in the complete streets movement, notably the Centers for Independent

Living and Easter Seals Project Action, which focuses on ensuring that the public transportation system is accessible for people with disabilities.

Under the Americans with Disabilities Act, jurisdictions of all kinds with more than fifty employees, including transportation agencies, are required to write transition plans that focus on ending access barriers for people with disabilities. The plans must solicit input from the community, set a timeline for action, and name someone responsible for implementation. A major component of almost all transportation agency transition plans is prioritizing the enormous job of installing curb ramps. The ADA, of course, predates the complete streets movement, and only a few places have integrated the plans with their complete streets commitment.

Since the complete streets approach is about serving everyone using the roads, some communities will identify some more unusual road users.[5] Communities with Amish populations or equestrian centers are making provisions for carriages or for unpaved paths to provide riders with access to parks. The Georgia DOT is including a tunnel as part of a bridge improvement project that will allow kayakers to carry their boats across a lake to reach a recreation center. Some communities with snowy winters have worked to ensure that snowmobilers can use wide shoulders to get into town in the winter. The fundamental principle is to pay attention to who will be using a road, and to be sure they have safe access.

Bicycle Riders

This is the constituency that started the complete streets movement and that has had the most passion and energy for wresting space and resources from the automobile. While highly visible in transportation debates, in the United States they usually have the smallest mode share. This is largely because, until recently, they had no street space at all. Riders were few because of the perceived risks of sharing the lane with cars and buses—and because riding on sidewalks with pedestrians doesn't work either. A few bicycle advocates have long argued that the best way to increase riding and safety is to teach people to ride comfortably with cars in traffic (called "vehicular cycling"), but the vast majority of advocates now are pushing for more dedicated space on the roadway. They base their work on international research that clearly shows that dedicated space is the key to increasing bicycle use. This is particularly true for women, who in the United

States make up only about one quarter of the tiny fraction of utilitarian cyclists. In countries with the most bicycle-friendly streets, and the highest share of trips by bicycle, this striking gender imbalance disappears.[6]

The League of American Bicyclists rewards a systematic approach to including bicycles in transportation planning through its Bicycle Friendly Communities program; a complete streets policy is required to gain top status.[7] Cities all over the country have been gradually adding painted bike lanes and trails for the past two decades, and a new generation of facilities is aimed at making riding a clearly safer option for people who otherwise wouldn't ride bicycles, especially children and families. The industry group Bikes Belong (made up of manufacturers and retail bike store owners) is promoting the Green Lane Project, an initiative to help cities install protected bike lanes, safer intersection treatments, and other innovations.[8] The growing political clout of the bicycle industry and the advocacy movement means more resources and more space.

Bicycling is reaching a tipping point, rapidly shifting from a marginal subculture of recreational riders and diehard male commuters into a significant mode of transportation. Nationally, the share of people who bike to work grew by 64 percent between 1990 and 2009, with far higher increases in many cities.[9] Identifying as a "bicyclist" is no longer even necessary: bikeshare systems—which rent bicycles in half-hour increments from kiosks placed throughout a city—eliminate the need to even own a bike. Opening in cities around the world, they function essentially as transit systems in which the vehicles are bicycles.

Much of this activity is in core cities, but bicycling's greatest potential may be in suburban areas where it is simply too far to walk from homes to other destinations or even to reach public transportation. Low-income workers already know this, but they travel under the radar of transportation experts. Barry Barker, of the Louisville transit agency, says that when he was preparing to put bike racks on the city's buses years ago, he would make jokes about serving "the spandex crowd." But once they were installed, he says, "what we quickly learned was the extent to which year-round, the bike is a form of transportation for minority, low income individuals in Louisville. This is probably the most significant thing we've done for access to jobs." Yet, the challenge in these areas remains creating safe space for bicycles when cars are traveling at high speed.

Public Transportation Riders

The complete streets movement is often assumed to be focused on making the streets work better for pedestrians and bicyclists. That is the biggest challenge, in the many places where there is no safe place at all for people on foot and bicycle. But public transportation stands to gain the most in the push and pull around who gets use of limited street space. In the shift to ensuring that streets are safe and efficient in moving people instead of vehicles, public transportation inevitably rises to the top: buses, trains, streetcars and light rail trains are the fastest way to carry the most people. For example, in one corridor in Washington, DC, planners estimate that buses make up just 2 percent of the vehicles but carry 40 percent of the people. And aside from crashes involving transit patrons during the pedestrian part of their trip, transit is also the safest way to travel. Transit vehicles can also be thought of as "pedestrian accelerators," a critical component of a truly walkable city.[10]

But buses and trains have a requirement fundamentally different from the pedestrians they serve: speed. They need to move quickly enough to be competitive with private cars. And while the calculations of the costs of traffic congestion for individual drivers are suspect, for transit agencies time really is money. Slower bus service means agencies must pay drivers more per route and must buy and run more buses to provide frequent service (and frequency is essential when trying to draw drivers out of their cars). Complete streets converges with the movement toward light rail and bus rapid transit, because both involve reallocating street space to the exclusive use of transit vehicles, retiming signals to give priority to transit, and enhancing pedestrian access to the stations.

Jarrett Walker, a public transportation consultant and author of *Human Transit*, believes that in some cases the success of public transportation will eventually depend on taking lanes from automobiles—even though he told me most DOTs still react to this idea as if "you're proposing to kill kittens." He says, "If transit were allowed to succeed, it would use that lane much more efficiently in terms of person through-put, and it would be reliable in a way that cars will never be." Walker argues in his book that the nation's surfeit of suburban arterials, with many destinations along a straight line, are in fact the perfect place to reallocate street space to allow buses fast, frequent, predictable travel.[11] This would require some dedicated lanes, relatively infrequent but carefully placed stops, and a safe pedestrian crossing at every stop. But it wouldn't mean converting that arterial into a classically "walkable" urban street—because slowing the street that much would also slow down transit service. Instead, Walker argues for a buffered pedestrian zone that is safe and functional.

Until very recently, the people who ride public transportation have generally not organized to push for more space on the street, and while low-income bus riders formed a successful "union" in Los Angeles, similar efforts have not been very successful elsewhere. Chicago's Active Transportation Alliance and New York's Transportation Alternatives advocate for public transportation improvements, as well as for walking and bicycling. In big cities where ridership is going up among younger people, transportation blogs and apps are giving voice to a desire for better service.

The American Public Transportation Association is a major supporter of the National Complete Streets Coalition and has worked to spread the word across the industry. But in most places, transit agencies have not been leading the charge for a higher priority on the street. These transit operators are most engaged with the challenge of running the buses and trains, day in and day out. Because of the historic siloed approach to transportation planning, they are also usually entirely separate agencies from those that plan and build the roads, with boundaries that don't coincide with city or even county lines. For them to assert any say over the road side of the equation is seen as invading someone else's turf.

But Walker says that city governments that want to solve their transportation problems with transit should not be shy about working directly to find more space for public transportation. Seattle wrote its own transit plan, even though the city does not run the bus service. The 2005 plan clarified what the city wanted from the regionwide transit agency, King County Metro, and became an important tool for Metro to use in providing better, more innovative service.[12]

Those Who Stay Put

Often, the people with the biggest influence on who gets road space are those who are most concerned with staying put: residents who live alongside a road, local business owners, and developers. Of course, they travel the roads too, but for my purposes their interests in space allocation have more to do with the ultimate character and impact of the project on their private property or livelihood. Usually defenders of the status quo, their visibility and political power mean they often dictate the pace of change.

Charlotte's Norm Steinman says that this is where the city's six-step planning process (described in chapter 4) breaks down. While the city has set a clear priority of creating a safer pedestrian environment, residents often completely oppose projects to install sidewalks or connect streets. "People would say, 'I don't care if it is six steps, eight steps, or two steps. I do not want the project,'" says Steinman. "So we're now working on different methods of public involvement to help us determine more quickly if it is going to be possible to get people in an affected area to support a project or not." His department has drawn up a risk matrix for different types of projects. Safety improvements that stay in the right-of-way, such as pedestrian refuge islands, are almost never opposed, but sidewalks that are perceived to infringe on private property are much more likely to spark opposition. These sidewalk projects now require a petition demonstrating that a majority of residents accepts them before they proceed. But Steinman and his staff are not giving up; their latest effort is to broaden public involvement beyond the residents to find and engage the travelers who will use the new facilities.

Developers whose business model relies on automobile access have also fought to maintain a focus on congestion relief and providing plenty of parking spaces, and highway building remains an important engine for sprawling development. But this may be changing, especially among developers, business owners, and city leaders who are recognizing that a different allocation of space can bring more business. Chris Leinberger, author of *The Option of Urbanism,* and Arthur C. Nelson, of the University of Utah, have both written extensively about the large-scale economic forces that are helping developers see a different route to profitability through mixed-use, transit-oriented developments, often termed new urbanism or smart growth.[13]

But business support is shifting on a small scale too—for example, real estate developers and other businesses along Portland's Multnomah

Street recently supported the reallocation of two automobile lanes along the road to create protected bike lanes. The businesses want more visibility on a street that had been marked by speeding traffic. They hope to get it from bicycle riders, slower-moving drivers, and an increase in people walking.[14] And they hope that in the long run, the new configuration will help transform a throughway into a desirable place. Such placemaking is driving the most radical reallocations of all: freeway teardowns that usually aim to turn waterfront corridors from speedways into attractive neighborhoods and destinations.

Shifting Space

Cleveland's Euclid Avenue shows the potential benefits of taking the issue of space allocation head-on. Euclid Avenue is a central commercial corridor for Cleveland, linking the central business district and the job center of University Circle; the street is home to the Cleveland Clinic, the

Cleveland's HealthLine reallocated space along Euclid Avenue,
dedicating two central lanes to rapid transit, adding transit stations,
and narrowing the remaining automobile lanes.
(Photo courtesy Jerome Masek / Cleveland RTA.)

University Hospital, and Cleveland State University. While the corridor had street cars decades ago, more recently it had a pretty standard cross section: along most of its length, it had four vehicle travel lanes, parking, and sidewalks. The need for better transit service was recognized as early as the 1980s, and the regional transit authority applied for and won federal "New Starts" funding for the HealthLine, a BRT line. The project ended up reconfiguring the street from curb to curb for eight miles: sidewalks were widened; 726 curbside parking spaces were moved off the street; and in some sections, additional right-of-way was acquired to make room for five-foot-wide bike lanes. Two central lanes are dedicated to the rapid transit vehicles, which are sped along by signal preemption and off-board fare collection. One through vehicle lane remains in each direction; the Ohio Department of Transportation approved a design exception to allow these to be narrowed to eleven feet. Some parts of the corridor have parking bays and turn lanes.

The Greater Cleveland Regional Transit Authority designed the entire project, even though the road is a state highway. Joe Calabrese, CEO and general manager, says his agency stood firm in talks with the city and state transportation agencies on how the corridor would look and operate, aided by the leverage provided by the federal funding. "We were bringing money to the table; we were bringing the promise of future economic vitality, which was crucial. Yes, we got away with a lot but we knew it was the right thing to do." His agency also worked with adjacent land owners block by block—and overcame the resistance of one group of developers who were sure that the revitalization of downtown depended on adding more parking.

Ridership on the line jumped 46 percent in the first year, and the bicycle count tripled between 2006 and 2010.[15] The project has been a huge boon to economic development; new housing and retail are going up in underdeveloped Midtown. And the doubtful developers? They are now building a mixed-use development with ground-floor retail and apartments above on the University Circle end of the corridor.

The Euclid Avenue story is an illustration of just how much a single street can be changed to give different modes different priorities, and how that can affect surrounding land use. But such transformations won't go nationwide if every project has to compete for the limited federal funding devoted to special transit projects. Los Angeles is building a citywide BRT system using sales tax dollars; the existing lines have already dramatically improved travel speeds and attracted many more riders.

Shifting Spending

As is the case with many ground-breaking projects, the HealthLine required an enormous effort and special funding. At the project level, achieving that perfect balance of capacity and convenience for each mode looks like a design challenge—and one that can too easily be pulled off course by political considerations. But as always with complete streets, the path to lasting change does not lie at the level of designing a single roadway. Complete streets policies require politicians and practitioners to realign priorities across the entire transportation network when allocating resources, space, and time.

The most important change an agency can make to achieve a better balance is to change the way it spends its money. As discussed in chapter 1, funding sources defined by mode are one of the reasons we have so many incomplete streets. Agencies default to fractured decision making—or, if they want to build multimodal solutions, they end up with a difficult dance of coordination. In the report *The Innovative DOT,* Smart Growth America and the State Smart Transportation Initiative recommend that states can get over this hurdle by eliminating mode-specific accounts, creating new mode-neutral funding streams, and creating targeted funds that help allocate money based on state priorities.[16] The first two strategies are at the core of the commitment made when a jurisdiction adopts a complete streets policy: ensuring that all transportation dollars are used to make the network safe for all travelers. For example, the complete streets law passed by the Wisconsin legislature made a clear policy statement, which was then integrated into the administrative rules governing street rehabilitation and construction, mandating that highway projects must include sidewalks and bike lanes. This takes the act of priority setting up one level: the policy means advocates for pedestrian and bicycle interests can shift their fight for space from "why" or "whether" to "how."

But updating existing mode-specific accounts is only a first step. Truly mode-neutral funding pots need to be eligible for public transportation projects, and need to prioritize safety for all users in the project selection process. A good early example of reworking funding pots to better serve local needs is the Sacramento Area Council of Governments (SACOG). California has suballocated much of its federal money to regional control, so Sacramento has been able to distribute federal funding into a structure tailored to fit the region's needs—and to respond to citizen pressure for a more balanced approach.[17] Several SACOG funding programs support multimodal projects, such as the Community Design Funding Program, the Air Quality Funding Program, and transportation demand management; a Bicycle Pedestrian Funding Program targets nonmotorized improvements. This system has been in place for well over a decade. In 2012, the SACOG board allocated 69 percent of its 2012 program to projects that primarily support transit, bicycle, or pedestrian travel. The region's priorities have shifted significantly since 2008, with bicycle and pedestrian programs getting the highest per capita funding increase in the master transportation plan. But advocates believe SACOG can do much more, by setting a target for increasing walking and bicycling trips and by setting a timetable for completing its streets—the California Complete Streets Coalition suggests a target date of 2024.[18]

Setting Criteria

Many agencies have created new systems to help them select and fund projects that will bring a better balance to their street network. New project prioritization systems are most common at the state and regional levels, and many agencies create points systems that reward multimodal inclusion or adjust an existing points system to favor multimodal projects. The North Carolina DOT has revamped its entire planning system to align its funding more closely with its goals, and part of that is a new project-scoring process. NCDOT is using different scoring systems for highway, transit, and nonmotorized projects, but highway projects include scoring criteria based on inclusion of transit options, multimodal connections, and design features that serve people on foot and bicycle.[19]

Metropolitan Planning Organizations have often approached their responsibility for distributing federal dollars as a stapling exercise: they collected funding requests from each city, county, and town and stapled them together for submittal. But many MPOs are now creating more rigorous project-selection systems. The Nashville MPO revamped the way it chose projects for inclusion in its long-range transportation plan, award-ing points for those that would improve air quality, active transportation options, physical activity, and safety; points were also awarded for proj-ects in "health impact areas," places that would benefit the most from healthy transportation options because of their high population of people of color, those with lower incomes, and older adults. Under the new plan adopted in 2010, 70 percent of the projects have some active transporta-tion infrastructure, compared with 2 percent of the projects in the plan adopted five years earlier.[20]

The Kansas City regional agency, the Mid-America Regional Council, created a sophisticated points system to select projects for inclusion in its long-range transportation plan—and made sure that it gave many in-terests a chance to weigh in. The overarching regional vision calls for "a safe, balanced, regional multimodal transportation system that is coordi-nated with land-use planning, supports equitable access to opportunities, and protects the environment." This vision was broken into nine specific goals. MARC staff scored more than five hundred projects submitted by the region's members. Committees of elected officials, local planners, and engineers were formed to represent the interests of each mode, and they identified gaps and refined priorities and scoring, all in the context of what the region could afford. The general public had several chances to comment as well. The end result: 90 percent of projects improve exist-ing facilities rather than building new, and 75 percent support projects in the region's identified activity centers.[21] This was a planning exercise; the long-range plan disburses no funds. But near-term projects should make it into the five-year transportation improvement program.

At the local level, complete streets policies often lead directly to new funding allocations. As discussed previously, taxpayers and elected officials in Nashville, Seattle, and Arlington County have given the go-ahead to funding programs that are explicitly multimodal. The changes in funding free up transportation agencies to step back and take a network approach.

When setting priorities on individual streets, the standard will never be "all modes for all roads." Every street won't be prioritized the same way for every user, but effective overlapping networks should be in place to help travelers get where they are going by whatever method, or combina-tion of methods, they choose. Boulder, Colorado, pioneered the mapping of such overlapping networks. Los Angeles is creating "Transit- and Bicycle-Enhanced" networks but has decided that pedestrian enhancements should be made on just about every street.

Taking Equity into Account

But project-selection systems have limitations, particularly when they lean toward technical criteria in a way that may lose track of the needs of the various types of people and vehicles using the street. Many agencies that have made a commitment to complete streets have focused on accommodating all modes but have done less to attend to the needs of the different abilities of the people using those modes. Paying attention to the needs of disadvantaged road users requires another level of prioritization, as discussed by Kelly Clifton and Sarah Bronstein in research conducted in cooperation with the National Complete Streets Coalition.[22]

In one of the case studies conducted for the study, they note that Portland, Oregon's celebrated work to create a more complete network still left out a significant part of the city. Bicycle and pedestrian plans in Portland had prioritized projects in technical terms, funding projects that served intensive land uses, those that served the highest volume of cyclists, and those that closed network gaps economically. While this approach helped infrastructure and use grow significantly in the central city and adjacent neighborhoods within the city's historic grid, residents of East Portland got less attention and experienced fewer benefits. East Portland has a higher portion of residents without good access to transportation, including children, older adults, people of color, and immigrants. It also has wider roads with higher speeds and longer blocks more hostile to nonmotorized travel. The area, with its more suburban development style, has proven more difficult to retrofit. While bike lanes were added, they were not really serving East Portland's high proportion of nondrivers, including older adults and children, and ridership did not rise as it did elsewhere in the city. The area has a median household income that is 23 percent lower than that in the rest of Portland, so clearly more travel options are important.

The health department used a health grant to research solutions, forming a broad-based review committee to guide the work. The committee found that much of the problem lay in the process used to choose projects: while equity policies already existed, they were vague and not incorporated into day-to-day decision making. The next edition of the city's transportation system plan adds in prioritization criteria that take into account the needs of the people being served. Specifically, the system will give points to projects that are located in a block group with higher-than-average underserved populations and that improve safety, reduce exposure to air pollution, and complete network gaps.

The Importance of Priorities

All of these systems help set priorities long before the issue comes down to the level of the individual street. But while they may help head off a brawl between drivers and bicyclists over whether to include a bike lane or a parking lane on a particular street, they don't eliminate the push and pull between different users of the street. As planners discovered when implementing the six-step process in Charlotte, planning systems have to be adjusted to take strong opposition into account. And political leadership is often the way that final decisions get made. But a systematic approach ensures that everyone's voice is heard—and gives the different entities vying for space and resources a focal point as they work for a different street environment.

While the setting of priorities can get complicated, the most important point is to simply be aware of the need to set them. Many jurisdictions begin their commitment to complete streets by adding sidewalks and bicycle lanes where they are sorely needed but not changing anything else about their automobile-oriented planning system. That's a great start. But if community leaders do not take the next step, if they do not look more closely at the needs of different travelers and revamp the way they prioritize serving them, they will end up attending meetings like the one I describe in the opening pages of this book. The residents of Montgomery County, Maryland, are frustrated with seemingly unsolvable safety problems, despite the County's robust pedestrian safety program. The County is spending millions building sidewalks and safe crossings and creating higher awareness. But the program can't make up for an unexamined decision-making system that still designs for automobile access first and considers other users only later—and, often, too late.

This approach results in costly, inefficient, and only partially effective attempts to build complete streets. Montgomery County has adopted a complete streets policy, and some things are changing—a few road conversions have been successful, and the County has conducted a nationally recognized upgrade of its bus stops and shelters. But consistent progress will come only when the County, and jurisdictions like it, start to examine and change the systems that keep producing incomplete streets.

Many communities are combining complete streets initiatives with "greening" their streets to better handle storm water runoff. (Photo courtesy Kevin Robert Perry.)

CHAPTER NINE

Expanding Complete Streets

I N THE DECADE SINCE the term *complete streets* was coined, hundreds of transportation agencies have woken up to the need to serve all users. Long-forecast demographic trends are starting to play out as the growing population of older adults seeks alternatives to driving and young people do the same. BRT, car sharing, and bike sharing have begun to come into their own. Urban areas with options are in; isolated suburbs are out.

Should complete streets evolve too? Some places are leading the way, going far beyond the basic complete streets concept, reworking their transportation systems, actively prioritizing pedestrians or public transportation, and all while contributing to environmental sustainability. All this may make complete streets seem a little old-fashioned; practitioners and advocates get impatient and wish for what they see as a more complete movement that will expand to encompass environmental concerns and directly tackle the land use changes that are necessary to create truly walkable, bikeable, transit-friendly communities.

In my experience, this search for a perfect policy is in fact an attempt to define a perfect future—and it won't do much good. No one initiative can—or should—be the single answer to the multiple problems presented by the way we've been building our communities for more than a half century.

Instead, I think it is important for complete streets to remain firmly rooted in where people are right now. And right now, most of them are not in Boulder or New York City. They still live in places without enough sidewalks, places where older adults, children, and low-income people are using "goat paths" as the cars whiz by. As complete streets steering committee member Randy Neufeld is fond of saying, the United States has more than thirty thousand local jurisdictions, and only about five hundred of these have made a commitment to complete streets.

The movement will keep growing if it continues to attract a wide range of people to support a sharply focused policy solution; the only criterion for getting on board is agreeing that the roads should be safe for everyone. The temptation to "update" complete streets to carry the weight of all the other changes that are desired is appealing to true believers—but it would greatly reduce the power to bring along communities where walking down the street is still a dangerous act, and where sustainability, smart growth, and livability are not widely shared values. In much of the United States, it is still a huge victory to simply "stop the bleeding" by ending the transportation agency practice of conducting its business as if people don't walk, ride buses or bikes, or have disabilities. The clear and narrow focus of the movement is a strength—it is why the complete streets movement is taking hold from Billings, Montana, to Birmingham, Alabama.

A better strategy is the one dozens of jurisdictions are pursuing: make complete streets, and the systemic, institutional changes it demands, one tine of a multipronged plan to change their communities for the better. In these places, transportation professionals take satisfaction in the small victory of safer streets, and also in their contribution to wider community goals.

Complete streets is easy to pair up with other initiatives: its narrow focus on a safer street environment can gain strength and depth when a community links it to a community desire to become more sustainable, to help more residents be active and healthy, or to create more compact and convenient communities. And some communities are doing all three, sometimes calling such an effort "Great Streets" or "Livable Streets."

Streets are impervious surfaces that speed storm water runoff, contributing to water pollution and flooding. So, some communities are creating combination complete-and-green street policies to further broaden the considerations when making transportation decisions. Boston's Complete Streets Guidelines include an extensive "green" component, as they seek to add street trees, permeable surfaces, and bioswales for drainage. In La Crosse, Wisconsin, city transportation director Larry Kirch realized that the way to bring the public works division on board was to connect complete streets to the City's need to create a storm water utility. He saw a connection between the approach of building ever-larger streets to move more cars and ever-larger pipes to handle storm water. Selling the "Green Complete Streets" ordinance was made easier by a recent street installation right outside the city council's doors. Kirch says, "We could just point out the window: this is what Green Complete Streets look like." Cities that are prioritizing green streets may work harder than most to avoid projects that require any additional street width, and may use road conversions and shared lanes, while experimenting with pervious pavements. Street trees have always been a core part of the complete streets concept because of their shade and traffic calming qualities.

If green streets are the micro level of environmental concern, slowing global climate disruption is the macro level—and complete streets works well with both. A number of big cities pursuing a complete streets approach are competing to become the greenest cities in America, or at least those with the lowest greenhouse gas emissions. Seattle, Boston, New York, and Chicago are all completing streets with an eye to creating mode shifts that will bring down emissions—and that means stretching to create biking, walking, and public transportation options that are not only safe but also lure people out of automobiles.

The public health goal of creating activity-friendly environments makes for complete streets initiatives that put a greater emphasis on changing personal behavior and connecting streets to trail networks. Nashville, Tennessee's complete streets initiative has been part of a much broader effort to help people eat well and get active. The Bicycle and Pedestrian Advisory Committee is engaged in complete streets implementation and is also very active in encouraging more biking and walking by establishing a bike-share system, publishing a map that helps bicyclists navigate the city's disconnected street network, and sponsoring bike corrals at major public events. The public works department has helped create the "Music City Bikeway," a twenty-six-mile route using trails, bike lanes, park roads, and shared roads to create bicycle connections across the city.

Complete streets can only do so much to create a multimodal network in places marked by spread-out subdivisions and stand-alone office parks, each accessible only from roads that branch off of big arterial streets.

Many places adopting a complete streets approach do so to support a big vision to create more compact communities that mix together shops, homes, and businesses on a more connected street network. Chapter 5 mentions some of the street-level attempts to do this through regulations guiding private development.

Long-range planning is another arena where communities are working to achieve smarter growth, and the complete streets approach plays an important supporting role. Charlotte, North Carolina, has established a regionwide plan to focus development into growth corridors that will be served by rapid transit while "wedge" areas will continue to host lower-density neighborhoods. The Sacramento region adopted its fifty-year blueprint for smarter growth in 2004, and its clear focus has helped redirect transportation investments in ways that create multimodal streets. Complete streets policies in these communities are a necessary part of this bigger picture, and they benefit from a longer vision and the broader commitment that will eventually result in truly walkable streets.

In looking at land use on a micro scale, some communities are working to ensure that the street itself is making an important contribution to community life. Most notably, New York City has been reallocating street space for people who want to stay awhile. The conversion of Times Square to a walkable area is most famous, but the city has put pocket parks in roads and intersections all over the city, in part to address the desperate need for more green space.[1] Even if streets are not converted for such uses, they can make a significant contribution to creating a sense of place. Jurisdictions that prioritize placemaking in their policies will closely align neighborhood and area plans with street improvements and will pay attention to the finer details.

But does the complete streets movement have much to offer to the cutting-edge communities that are reaching far beyond a basic safety goal? The concept by itself may no longer offer these places inspiration, but the change model offers instruction for the more ambitious changes they seek. In his book *The Tipping Point*, Malcolm Gladwell says that change comes at the margins. It isn't about simply doing more of the thing you want to change; it is about finding the small factors that will help "tip" the balance to create fundamental transformation. Changing the way we build our communities requires something more than coming up with the perfect design template or even a new policy proposal. The success of the complete streets movement shows how important it is to reframe the way we think and talk about long-standing built environment issues. It demonstrates that building political will is important both when a policy is being debated and when it is time for agencies to put it into practice. And it shows that institutional change requires spending less time defining an ideal future and more time understanding the present in order to build a solid path that leads gradually to better results. These lessons apply whether a community is working toward routine installation of sidewalks or is seeking acceptance of a forward-looking form-based planning code. Complete streets, and the three key strategies that define its success, maintain the power to transform.

Case Study Finder

For more information on many of the communities mentioned in this book, please refer to the full case studies listed below in **bold**. Case studies for other communities pursuing complete streets solutions are listed in plain text. The capital letters indicate the source, with full source information at the end of the list. Those in sources B through E are case studies that the author wrote or edited.

Atlanta Regional Commission: H
Ann Arbor, MI: F
Arlington County, VA: E, F, G
Baldwin Park, CA: D
Boise, ID: F
Boston, MA: B, E
Boulder, CO: E
California DOT: C
Charlotte, NC: E, F, E, G, K
Chicago, IL: E
Cleveland, OH: M
Colorado Springs, CO: E
Columbia, MO: E
Columbus, OH: E
Davis, CA: D
Decatur, GA: A, E
East-West Gateway COG, St. Louis, MO: E
Florida DOT: E
Fort Collins, CO: E
Hawaii DOT: C
Hoboken, NJ: F
Kansas City, MO: G
Kauai County, HI: B
Kirkland, WA: E
La Crosse, WI: B
Lancaster, CA: D
Los Angeles, CA: F
Louisville, KY: B, E
Massachusetts DOT: C, E, I

Minneapolis, MN: E
Minnesota DOT: C, G, H, I
Nashville, TN: A, B, J
New Haven, CT: E
New Jersey DOT: C, G, H
New York City: E, F, G, K
North Carolina DOT: H
Olympia, WA: E
Oregon DOT: E, H
Pennsylvania DOT: E, G, H
Pierce County, WA: E
Portland, OR: A
Redmond, WA: E, K
Roanoke, VA: E
Rochester, MN: B, E
Sacramento, CA: D, E, K
San Diego County/City, CA: B, D, E,
   F, J, L
San Francisco (city), CA: D, G
San Francisco MPO (Bay Area), CA: E, H
San Jose, CA: G
Santa Barbara, CA: E
Santa Monica, CA: D
Seattle, WA: E, G, K
Sault Ste. Marie, MI: A
University Place, WA: E
Virginia DOT: E
Washtenaw County, MI: E

A: Clifton, Kelly, Sarah Bronstein, and Sara Morrissey. *The Path to Complete Streets in Underserved Communities: Lessons from U.S. Case Studies.* Portland, OR: Portland State University, 2013. http://www.smartgrowthamerica.org/documents/cs/resources/complete-streets-in-underserved-communities.pdf.

B: McCann, Barbara. *Taking Action on Complete Streets: Implementating Processes for Safe, Multimodal Streets.* National Complete Streets Coalition/Centers for Disease Control and Prevention, June 2013.

C: Seskin, Stefanie, and Barbara McCann. *Complete Streets in the States: A Guide to Legislative Action.* Washington, DC: AARP, January 2013. http://www.smartgrowthamerica.org/documents/cs/resources/cs-aarp-statelegislationtoolkit.pdf.

D: McCann, Barbara, Adam Meyer, Jenny Woods, and Chris Morfas. *It's a Safe Decision: Complete Streets in California.* Washington, DC: National Complete Streets Coalition and Local Government Commission, 2012. http://www.smartgrowthamerica.org/2012/02/28/complete-streets-success-stories-focus-of-new-report.

E: McCann, Barbara, and Suzanne Rynne. *Complete Streets: Best Policy and Implementation Practices.* Planners Advisory Service Report 559. Chicago: American Planning Association, 2010. http://www.planning.org/research/streets.

F: Walsh, Ryan. *Local Policies and Practices That Support Safe Pedestrian Environments: A Synthesis of Highway Practice.* National Cooperative Highway Research Program Synthesis 436. Washington, DC: Transportation Research Board, 2012. http://apps.trb.org/cmsfeed/TRBNetProjectDisplay.asp?ProjectID=2947.

G: *Steps to a Walkable Community: A Guide for Citizens, Planners, and Engineers.* New York: Sam Schwartz Engineering and America Walks, 2012. http://americawalks.org/2012/09/america-walks-and-sam-schwartz-engineering-release-steps-to-a-walkable-community. This report includes numerous one-page case studies; only those directly relevant to this book are listed here.

H: *The Innovative DOT: A Handbook of Policy and Practice.* Washington, DC: Smart Growth America and State Smart Transportation Initiative, 2012. http://www.smartgrowthamerica.org/the-innovative-dot.

I: Shinkle, Douglas, Jaime Rall, and Alice Wheet. *On the Move: State Strategies for 21st Century Transportation Solutions.* Washington, DC: National Conference of State Legislatures, 2012. http://www.ncsl.org/documents/transportation/On-THE-MOVE.pdf.

J: *Healthier Americans for a Healthier Economy: Issue Brief.* Washington, DC: Trust for America's Health, October 2011. http://tfah.org/assets/files/TFAH2011PreventEconomy05.pdf.

K: Ferrier, Kathleen, Andy Hamilton, and Greg Konar. *Safe for All: 2011 Street Design Benchmark Study for the San Diego Region.* San Diego, CA: Walk San Diego, 2011. http://www.walksandiego.org.

L: Jones, Michael G., et al. *Measuring Bicycle and Pedestrian Activity in San Diego County and Its Relationship to Land Use, Transportation, Safety, and Facility Type.* Berkeley: University of California, Berkeley, Safe Transportation Research and Education Center, 2010. http://www.altaplanning.com/caltrans+seamless+study.aspx.

M: *Transit as Transformation: The Euclid Corridor in Cleveland.* Case study. Washington, DC: Partnership for Sustainable Communities, 2012. http://www.sustainablecommunities.gov/pdf/studies/cleveland-euclid-corridor.pdf.

Complete Streets Resources

The National Complete Streets Coalition maintains extensive resources for those looking for information and assistance in pursuing adoption of complete streets policies and help with implementation. Here are a few highlights; more are available at http://www.smart growthamerica.org/complete-streets.

Complete Streets Fundamentals
Benefits of Complete Streets. Downloadable PowerPoint file summarizing the benefits of complete streets.
http://www.smartgrowthamerica.org/complete-streets /complete-streets-fundamentals/benefits-of-complete-streets/#presentation

Fact Sheets. Two-page, printable fact sheets on the benefits of a complete streets approach to the following populations and issues:
Children
People with Disabilities
Older Adults
Health
Public Transportation
Climate Change
Economic Revitalization
Gas Prices
Safety
Lower Transportation Costs
Create Livable Communities
View the web versions at the link below to see many associated resources listed at the bottom of each page.
http://www.smartgrowthamerica.org/complete-streets /complete-streets-fundamentals/factsheets

Changing Policy: Policy Writing and Adoption
Policy Development. Downloadable PowerPoint presentation on how to develop a policy.
http://www.smartgrowthamerica.org/complete-streets/changing-policy

Atlas. Track policy growth and look up policies in your state.
http://www.smartgrowthamerica.org/complete-streets/changing-policy /complete-streets-atlas

Complete Streets Policy Analysis. Report (issued annually in the spring) ranks every written policy in the United States.
http://www.smartgrowthamerica.org/documents/cs/cs-policyanalysis.pdf

Complete Streets Local Policy Workbook. Provides a step-by-step guide to the ten elements of an effective complete streets policy.
http://www.smartgrowthamerica.org/guides
/complete-streets-local-policy-workbook

Complete Streets in the States: A Guide to Legislative Action. Provides model policy language tailored to the state level, as well as strategic discussion.
http://www.smartgrowthamerica.org/complete-streets/changing-policy
/model-policy/model-state-legislation

Complete Streets Implementation

Resources are available on the four steps of policy implementation as well as on planning for implementation. Watch the page below for updated resources on the costs of complete streets and a new case study report, *Taking Action on Complete Streets: Implementing Processes for Safe, Multimodal Streets.*
http://www.smartgrowthamerica.org/complete-streets/implementation

The Path to Complete Streets in Underserved Communities: Lessons from U.S. Case Studies. Case studies and findings on how complete streets can serve low-income, senior, and other disadvantaged populations.
http://www.smartgrowthamerica.org/documents/cs/resources/complete-streets-in
-underserved-communities.pdf

Fact Sheets. Two-page, printable fact sheets on the following implementation issues:
Ease Traffic Woes
Costs of Complete Streets
Change Travel Patterns
Complete and Green Streets
Networks of Complete Streets
Rural Areas and Small Towns
View the web versions at the following link to see many associated resources listed at the bottom of each page.
http://www.smartgrowthamerica.org/complete-streets/implementation/fact-sheets

Get Help

If your community is ready for more in-depth assistance, the Coalition offers workshops, technical assistance, and a list of consulting firms that take a complete streets approach.
http://www.smartgrowthamerica.org/complete-streets/get-help

Get Involved

The work of the National Complete Streets Coalition is supported by individuals, public interest groups, consulting firms, and other organizations. You can join the Coalition, sign up for the newsletter, schedule a workshop, and more at the "Get Involved" page.
http://www.smartgrowthamerica.org/complete-streets/get-involved

Endnotes

Preface

1. Ewing et al., "Relationship between Urban Sprawl and Physical Activity, Obesity, and Morbidity."
2. McCann and Ewing, *Measuring the Health Effects of Sprawl.*

Introduction

1. Smart Growth America, "National Complete Streets Coalition: Policy Atlas," http://www.smartgrowthamerica.org/complete-streets/changing-policy/complete-streets-atlas. Check this map to see the current status of policy adoption across the United States.
2. Smart Growth America, "National Complete Streets Coalition: Newsletter," http://www.smartgrowthamerica.org/complete-streets/newsletter. The evidence of complete streets activity across the country is easy to follow in the National Complete Streets Coalition's monthly e-newsletter.
3. Fairbank, Maslin, Maullin, Metz & Associates and Public Opinion Strategies, "Key Findings from National Survey on Transportation Options," August 3, 2012, http://docs.nrdc.org/energy/files/ene_12090401a.pdf.
4. Nelson, *Reshaping Metropolitan America*, 33–46.

Chapter One

1. *Highway Statistics 2010* (Washington, DC: Federal Highway Administration, 2011), table HM-20, Public Road Length 2010, http://www.fhwa.dot.gov/policy information/statistics/2010/hm20.cfm.
2. Greg Gordon and Curtis Tate, "Politics and Road Building Intersect in Kentucky," *McClatchy Newspapers*, February 3, 2013, http://www.mcclatchydc.com. In the same series, see "Special-Interest Push for South Carolina Interstate Hits Roadblock."
3. Huang et al., "A Systems-Oriented Multilevel Framework for Addressing Obesity in the 21st Century."
4. A number of books have done a great job discussing the history and rise of transportation and land use planning in the United States. See Lewis, *Divided Highways*; Baldwin, *Fighting Traffic*; Jackson, *Crabgrass Frontier*; and Southworth and Ben-Joseph, *Streets and the Shaping of Towns and Cities.*
5. Jaffe, "The Transportation Planning Rule Every City Should Reform"; Tumlin, *Sustainable Transportation Planning*, 264–70.
6. Doug Short, "Vehicle Miles Driven: Population-Adjusted Hits Yet Another Post-Crisis Low," Dshort.com Advisor Perspectives (April 22, 2013), http://advisorperspectives.com/dshort/updates/DOT-Miles-Driven.php. See also the FHWA Traffic Volume Trends website for the original data source: http://www.fhwa.dot.gov/policy information/travel_monitoring/tvt.cfm.

7. See Smart Growth America and State Smart Transportation Initiative, *The Innovative DOT.*

Chapter Two

1. You can learn more about writing a complete streets policy at the National Complete Streets Coalition website: http://www.completestreets.org.

2. "City of St. Louis Aldermen Adopt Complete Streets," Trailnet news release, June 16, 2010, http://www.smartgrowthamerica.org/documents/cs/media/cs-trailnet-st louis-061610.pdf.

3. US Department of Transportation, "A Guide to Metropolitan Transportation Planning under ISTEA—How the Pieces Fit Together" (undated), http://ntl.bts.gov /DOCS/424MTP.html.

4. "Epic Meeting, Complete Streets Passes," December 20, 2011, Councilman Jon Snyder's blog, December 20, 2011, http://councilmanjonsnyder.com/. Post accessed February 6, 2013; no longer available.

5. National Complete Streets Coalition, "Steering Committee," http://www.smart growthamerica.org/complete-streets/who-we-are/steering-committee.

6. Rogers, *Diffusion of Innovations.*

7. Smith and Larimer, *The Public Policy Theory Primer.*

8. Gladwell, *The Tipping Point.*

9. Under the Policy-Systems-Environmental change model for complete streets, the "policy" is obvious; the "system" that must be changed is the process used to choose, plan, and build roads (sometimes called the "transportation project delivery system"), and the "environment" is the street. Most of this book focuses on the middle phase of the PSE model: the processes and practices of transportation agencies.

10. Wykle, *Accommodating Bicycle and Pedestrian Travel.*

11. McCann, *Complete Streets Report.*

12. Seskin and Gordon-Koven, *The Best Complete Streets Policies of 2012.*

13. For followers of Malcolm Gladwell's *The Tipping Point,* this is akin to what Gladwell calls "the law of the few." Spreading change is not scattershot; the targets of change need to connect with trustworthy people who can effectively deliver the message.

14. The complete streets approach has been discussed in Europe, Australia, New Zealand, and even China—but the National Complete Streets Coalition has focused its energies on developing the movement to fit the US context.

15. "Nickerson Street Project Improves Safety," City of Seattle press release (March 1, 2012), http://mayormcginn.seattle.gov/nickerson-street-project-improves-safety.

16. New York City Department of Transportation, "Executive Summary," in *Sustainable Streets Index 2011,* http://www.nyc.gov/html/dot/html/about/ssi.shtml.

17. Litman, *Short and Sweet.*

18. Pratt et al., "Pedestrian and Bicycle Facilities."

19. Rodriguez, *Active Transportation.*

20. Frank et al., *An Assessment of Urban Form and Pedestrian and Transit Improvements as an Integrated GHG Reduction Strategy.*

21. Los Angeles County Metropolitan Transportation Authority, "Final Report: Los Angeles Metro Rapid Demonstration Program" (March 2002), http://www.metro.net /projects_studies/rapid/images/demonstration_program_report.pdf.

22. Neil Maizlish et al., "Health Cobenefits and Transportation-Related Reductions in Greenhouse Gas Emissions in the San Francisco Bay Area," 706.

Chapter Three

1. *Complete Streets Legislative Report* (Honolulu: Hawaii Department of Transportation, 2012).
2. "Senate Transportation Committee Looks into Highway and Road Designs," Hawaii Senate Transportation and International Affairs Committee, March 13, 2012, http://www.capitol.hawaii.gov/committeepage.aspx?comm=TIA.
3. Connecticut Bicycle and Pedestrian Advisory Board, *2011 Annual Report* (2012), http://www.ctbikepedboard.org/uploads/1/0/3/8/10385744/annual_report_2011_ctbpab.pdf.
4. See http://www.smartgrowthamerica.org/complete-streets/changing-policy.
5. Seskin, *Complete Streets Policy Analysis 2011*.
6. For details and links, see Seskin, *Complete Streets Policy Analysis 2011*; and Seskin and Gordon-Koven, *The Best Complete Streets Policies of 2012*.
7. Urgo et al., *Moving beyond Prevailing Street Design Standards*.
8. Wieters et al., "Why Should We Care about Those Silly Pedestrians and Bicyclists?"
9. Centers for Disease Control and Prevention, "Protect the Ones You Love: Child Injuries Are Preventable," http://www.cdc.gov/safechild/NAP/background.html.
10. Transportation for America, *Dangerous by Design*.
11. Marshall and Garrick, "Street Network Types and Road Safety."
12. Ewing and Dumbaugh, "The Built Environment and Traffic Safety."
13. Jacobsen, "Safety in Numbers."
14. Federal Highway Administration, "Evaluation of Lane Reduction 'Road Diet' Measures on Crashes."
15. Tony Furst, *Guidance Memorandum on Promoting the Implementation of Proven Safety Countermeasures* (Federal Highway Administration Office of Safety, January 2012), http://safety.fhwa.dot.gov/provencountermeasures.
16. Potts et al., "Relationship of Lane Width to Safety for Urban and Suburban Arterials."
17. Scott Crawford, "Citizens Endangered by Lack of User Friendly Streets," *Jackson Clarion-Ledger*, April 15, 2012, http://www.clarionledger.com/article/20120416/OPINION/204160307/Citizens-endangered-by-lack-user-friendly-streets.
18. Safe42.org, "Order to Proceed Issued by Mayor Fischer," press release, June 1, 2012, http://www.safe42.org/order-to-proceed.

Chapter Four

1. Bleier et al., *From Policy to Pavement*.
2. Barbara McCann, *Taking Action on Complete Streets* (National Complete Streets Coalition/Centers for Disease Control and Prevention, forthcoming 2013). A number of the examples in this chapter are discussed more fully in this publication; see appendix A.
3. Los Angeles County, *Model Design Manual for Living Streets*.
4. Minnesota Department of Transportation, "Complete Streets Work Plan," March 15, 2013, http://www.dot.state.mn.us/planning/completestreets/docs/csworkplan.pdf.
5. National Complete Streets Coalition, *Getting Results: Complete Streets in Minnesota*.
6. While the FHWA has praised California's approach to CMAQ as a best practice, few other states have adopted it.
7. McCann et al., *The Regional Response to Federal Funding for Bicycle and Pedestrian Projects: Executive Summary*.
8. City of Seattle, Ordinance 122386, adopted April 30, 2007, http://www.seattle.gov/transportation/completeStreets.htm.
9. Carmalt, *Constructing, Maintaining and Financing Sidewalks in New Jersey*, 6.

10. Keila Szpaller, "New Way to Pay for Missoula Sidewalks to Go before City Council," *Missoulian*, September 21, 2012.

11. Tumlin, *Sustainable Transportation Planning*, 263–85. This chapter includes a comprehensive discussion of the options for a multimodal Level of Service standard.

12. Sam Schwartz Engineering and America Walks, *Steps to a Walkable Community*, 85.

13. Charlotte Department of Transportation, *Urban Street Design Guidelines* (2007), chap. 3.

14. "Sacramento Council of Governments Complete Streets Toolkit," http://www.sacog .org/complete-streets/toolkit/start.html.

15. Mid-America Regional Council, *Complete Streets Handbook*, 1.

16. Los Angeles County, *Model Design Manual for Living Streets*.

17. Institute for Transportation Engineers, *Designing Walkable Urban Thoroughfares*; National Association of City Transportation Officials, *Urban Bikeway Design Guide* and *Urban Street Design Guide* (forthcoming).

18. American Association of State Highway and Transportation Officials, *A Policy on Geometric Design of Highways and Streets*.

19. See http://www.dot.ca.gov/hq/tpp/offices/ocp/complete_streets.html.

20. McCann and Rynne, *Complete Streets: Best Policy and Implementation Practices*, 36.

21. City of Nashville, *Major and Collector Street Plan*.

22. See City of Philadelphia Streets Department, *Philadelphia Complete Streets Design Handbook*; San Francisco Planning Department, "San Francisco Better Streets Plan"; Boston Transportation Department, "Boston Complete Streets Guidelines"; Los Angeles County, *Model Design Manual for Living Streets*; and City of Chicago, *Complete Streets Chicago*.

23. Active Transportation Alliance, *Complete Streets: Complete Networks*.

24. City of Chicago, *Complete Streets Chicago*, 14.

25. City of Dallas, *Complete Streets Design Manual*.

26. City of Philadelphia Streets Department, *Philadelphia Complete Streets Design Handbook*.

27. For more information, see "Schedule a Workshop" at http://www.smartgrowth america.org/complete-streets/get-help/workshops.

28. "Complete Streets Memphis" (http://www.youtube.com/watch?v=hg_zFaW4xas) is just one example.

29. Aultman-Hall et al., "Innovative Data Collection for Pedestrians, Bicycles, and Other Non–Motor Vehicle Modes," 8.

30. Seattle Department of Transportation, *Bridging the Gap Annual Report 2011*, http:// www.seattle.gov/transportation/BridgingtheGap.htm.

31. "National Bicycle and Pedestrian Documentation Project," http://www.walkinginfo .org/library/details.cfm?id=4313.

32. Smart Growth America and State Smart Transportation Initiative, *The Innovative DOT*, 48.

33. City of Boulder Transportation Division, *Transportation to Sustain a Community: A Report on Progress* (February 2012), http://www.bouldercolorado.gov/files /Transportation/Transportation_Report_on_Progress_2012.pdf.

34. For a discussion of the various uses of performance measures, see McCann and Rynne, *Complete Streets: Best Policy and Implementation Practices*, 54–63.

Chapter Five

1. Walsh, *Local Policies and Practices That Support Safe Pedestrian Environments*. See chapter 2 for a discussion of the breadth of changes that can be made.

2. Virginia Transportation Research Council, *Survey of Statewide Multimodal Transport*

Planning Practices, National Cooperative Highway Research Program 404 (2002), http://onlinepubs.trb.org/onlinepubs/nchrp/nchrp_rpt_404.pdf.

3. Minnesota Department of Transportation, "Complete Streets Work Plan," March 15, 2013, 1, http://www.dot.state.mn.us/planning/completestreets/docs/csworkplan .pdf.

4   Kastenhofer, *An Examination of Practices for Retrofitting Existing Roads with Sidewalks in the United States*, 4.

5   Shapard and Cole, "Do Complete Streets Cost More than Incomplete Streets?"

6. For more information, see the website of the Form-Based Code Institute, http:// www.formbasedcodes.org.

7. American Association of State Highway and Transportation Officials, *Rough Roads Ahead*.

8. Shoup et al., *The Fix We're in For*.

9. See *Repair Priorities*.

10. Active Transportation Alliance, Write of Way weblog, "Complete Streets Policies in Action," blog post, August 29, 2012, http://www.activetrans.org/blog/barbcornew /complete-streets-policy-leads-newly-installed-bike-lane-des-plaines.

11. North Carolina Department of Transportation (NCDOT), *NCDOT Complete Streets Planning and Design Guidelines*.

12. NCDOT, *NCDOT Complete Streets Planning and Design Guidelines*, 143.

13. Grant et al., *The Role of Transportation Systems Management and Operations*.

14. Grant et al., *The Role of Transportation Systems Management and Operations*, 36.

15. Weinstein Agrawal, Nixon, and Murthy, *What Do Americans Think about Federal Tax Options to Support Public Transit, Highways, and Local Streets and Roads?*, 11.

Chapter Six

1. Barbara McCann, *Taking Action on Complete Streets* (National Complete Streets Coalition/Centers for Disease Control and Prevention, forthcoming 2013). A number of the examples in this chapter are discussed more fully in this publication; see appendix A.

2. Walsh, *Local Policies and Practices That Support Safe Pedestrian Environments*.

3. James Simpson, "N.J. Complete Streets Policy Paves Way for Road Safety," *Times of Trenton*, op-ed, November 18, 2011, http://www.state.nj.us/transportation/eng /completestreets/editorial.shtm.

4. Walkable and Livable Communities Institute, *Walkability Workbook* (April 2012), http://www.walklive.org/project/walkability-workbook; Mark Fenton's website, http://www.markfenton.com.

5. Center for Transportation Excellence, "Transportation Measures Continue Trend of Success on Election Day Coast-to-Coast, Voters Choose to Invest in Transit," press release, November 7, 2012, http://www.cfte.org/pages/2012presspost.

6. Natural Resources Defense Council, "Key Findings from National Survey on Transportation Options," press release, August 3, 2012, http://docs.nrdc.org/energy/files /ene_12090401a.pdf.

7. All sources in this paragraph are listed in National Complete Streets Coalition, *Costs of Complete Streets: What We Are Learning from State and Local Governments* (undated), http://www.smartgrowthamerica.org/documents/cs/factsheets/cs-costs-2.pdf.

8. Nashville Area Metropolitan Planning Organization, *2010 Nashville Area Regional Transportation Study* (2010).

9. Ferrier et al., *Safe for All*.

10. Bleier et al., *From Policy to Pavement*.

11. Guy Busby, "Some Fairhope Residents Complain about New Street System," *Mobile Press-Register*, March 18, 2012, http://blog.al.com/live/2012/03/some_residents _complain_about.html.

12. Rena Cutler, "Commissioner's Panel: Raising the Bar: Building Political Capital to Implement Key Design Initiatives" (NACTO Designing Cities conference, New York City, October 24, 2012), http://vimeo.com/55304860.

13. Centers for Disease Control and Prevention, "Community Profile: Nashville/David-son County, Tennessee," http://www.cdc.gov/CommunitiesPuttingPreventionto Work/communities/profiles/obesity-tn_nashville-davidson-county.htm.

14. Cortright, *Driven Apart*, 7.

15. Toth, *A Citizen's Guide to Better Streets*, 61.

16. Cortright, *Driven Apart*. Cortright provides a more formal critique of congestion research.

17. For more information, see the Team Better Blocks website, http://teambetterblock .com.

Chapter Seven

1   McCann and Seskin, *Complete Streets: Guide to Tackling the Cost Question*. Much of the information in this chapter is available in a different format, via this guide and its companion PowerPoint presentation.

2. Tomer, *Transit Access and Zero-Vehicle Households*.

3. For a gallery of such images, see "Dangerous Streets," http://www.flickr.com /photos/t4america/sets/72157622516593443.

4   U.S. PIRG Education Fund, *Do Roads Pay for Themselves?*

5. National Complete Streets Coalition and Local Government Commission, *It's a Safe Decision*.

6. Paula Reeves, "Developing and Implementing Complete Streets Program: Washington State" (presentation at Complete Streets Peer Exchange, November 16, 2011, Washington, DC).

7. Seskin, *Complete Streets Local Policy Workbook*, 24.

8. Shapard and Cole, "Do Complete Streets Cost More than Incomplete Streets?"

9   James K. Hartman, "Budget Memo #25: Neighboring Jurisdictions Use of Commercial Transportation Add-on Tax Funds," City of Alexandria, VA, memorandum (March 23, 2011), http://alexandriava.gov/uploadedFiles/budget/info/budget2012/memos /BM25NeighboringJurisdictionsUseOfCommercialTransportationAddOnTax.pdf.

10. National Complete Streets Coalition (NCSC), "Complete Streets Make for a Good Ride," NCSC fact sheet, http://www.smartgrowthamerica.org/documents/cs /factsheets/cs-transit.pdf.

11. Transportation for America, *Dangerous by Design*.

12. Dannenberg et al., *Making Healthy Places*; Frumkin et al., *Urban Sprawl and Public Health*; Active Living Research, "Research Briefs and Syntheses," http://www.active livingresearch.org/toolsandresources/researchbrief.

13 Trust for America's Health, *F as in Fat: How Obesity Threatens America's Future 2012* (September 2012), http://healthyamericans.org/report/100.

14. California Center for Public Health Advocacy, *The Economic Costs of Overweight, Obesity and Physical Inactivity among California Adults—2006* (July 9, 2009), http://www.public healthadvocacy.org/costofobesity.html.

15. Rodriguez, *Active Transportation*, 4.

16. Virginia Sisiopiku, Shah Imran, and Abdul Muqueet Abro, *Impacts of Transit in a*

Complete-Streets Context, UTCA Report Number 11206 (University Transportation Center for Alabama, April 2012), http://trid.trb.org/view/2012/M/1141068.

17. Trust for America's Health, *Healthier Americans for a Healthier Economy: Issue Brief* (October 2011), http://tfah.org/assets/files/TFAH2011PreventEconomy05.pdf.
18. Cortright, *Portland's Green Dividend*.
19. Litman, *Evaluating Non-motorized Transportation Benefits and Costs*.
20. New York City Department of Transportation, *Measuring the Street*.
21. Leinberger and Alfonzo, *Walk This Way*.
22. Partnership for Sustainable Communities, *Transit as Transformation: The Euclid Corridor in Cleveland* (case study, June 2012), http://www.sustainablecommunities.gov/pdf/studies/cleveland-euclid-corridor.pdf.
23. Geller, *How Portland Benefits from Bicycle Transportation*.
24. Arlington County Commuter Services Research Team, *ACCS Making an Impact FY 2011* (August 2012), http://mobilitylab.org/2012/08/15/accs-making-an-impact-fy2011.
25. Litman, *Evaluating Complete Streets*.
26. Eric Sundquist, "MassDOT Seeks to Triple Transit, Bike and Walk Share," *Springfield Republican*, October 15, 2012.
27. Eric Dumbaugh, "Rethinking the Economics of Traffic Congestion," *Atlantic Cities*, June 1, 2012, http://www.theatlanticcities.com/commute/2012/06/defense-congestion/2118.

Chapter Eight

1. Federal Highway Administration, *Summary of Travel Trends*.
2. Tina Trinkner, "Gabe Klein Pursues a Pedestrian-Friendly Message in Chicago," *Governing Magazine*, December 2011, http://www.governing.com/topics/transportation-infrastructure/gabe-klein-pursues-pedestrian-friendly-message-chicago.html.
3. Lynott et al., *Planning Complete Streets for an Aging America*.
4. National Complete Streets Coalition (NCSC), *Complete Streets Help Keep Kids Safe* (fact sheet, undated), http://www.smartgrowthamerica.org/documents/cs/factsheets/cs-children.pdf.
5. After initial uncertainty about whether it represented a wholly new mode, the Segway has become part of the mix on sidewalks in most communities, following a robust campaign by its makers to change state laws. It has not factored in many complete streets discussions.
6. Jan Garrard, Susan Handy, and Jennifer Dill, "Women and Cycling," in Pucher and Buehler, eds., *City Cycling*, 215.
7. League of American Bicyclists, "Bicycle Friendly Communities Program," http://www.bikeleague.org/programs/bicyclefriendlyamerica/communities.
8. Bikes Belong, "Green Lane Project: Sensible Solutions for City Streets," http://www.bikesbelong.org/bikes-belong-foundation/green-lane-project.
9. Alliance for Biking and Walking, *Bicycling and Walking in the United States*, 42.
10. Walker, *Human Transit*, 214.
11. Walker, *Human Transit*, 205–14.
12. Seattle Department of Transportation, "2005 Seattle Transit Plan," http://www.seattle.gov/transportation/transitnetwork.htm.
13. Leinberger, *The Option of Urbanism*; Nelson, *Reshaping Metropolitan America*.
14. Michael Andersen, "How Economic Growth Sold Portland Landlords on a Bikeway," *Green Lane Project Blog*, January 6, 2013, http://greenlaneproject.org/blog/view/how-the-promise-of-economic-growth-sold-portland-landlords-on-a-bikeway.

15. Partnership for Sustainable Communities, *Transit as Transformation: The Euclid Corridor in Cleveland* (case study, 2012), http://www.sustainablecommunities.gov/pdf/studies/cleveland-euclid-corridor.pdf.
16. Smart Growth America and State Smart Transportation Initiative, *The Innovative DOT*, 31.
17. Handy et al., *The Regional Response to Federal Funding for Bicycle and Pedestrian Projects.*
18. Sacramento Area Council of Governments, *Response to MTP/SCS Letter 32—Complete Streets Coalition of Sacramento*, March 16, 2012.
19. North Carolina Department of Transportation, "Strategic Prioritization" web page; see Prioritization 1.0 Highway Scoring Matrix, https://connect.ncdot.gov/projects/planning/Pages/StrategicPrioritization.aspx.
20. "Nashville Area 2035 Regional Transportation Plan: Impacts of Transportation Policy on Prevention and Health," http://www.nashvillempo.org/docs/Health/Health Summary_June2012.pdf.
21. Mid-America Regional Council, "Selecting Future Transportation Projects" (undated), http://www.marc.org/2040/Projects/selectionprocess.aspx.
22. Clifton et al., *The Path to Complete Streets in Underserved Communities*; Clifton et al., "The Adoption of Complete Streets in Transportation-Disadvantaged Communities."

Chapter Nine

1. Harnik, *Urban Green*, 131–53.

Selected Bibliography

Active Transportation Alliance. *Complete Streets: Complete Networks*. Chicago: Active Transportation Alliance, October 2012. http://www.atpolicy.org/Design.

Alliance for Biking and Walking. *Bicycling and Walking in the United States: 2012 Benchmarking Report*. Washington, DC, 2012.

American Association of State Highway and Transportation Officials (AASHTO). *A Policy on Geometric Design of Highways and Streets*. 6th ed. Washington, DC: AASHTO, 2011.

——. *Rough Roads Ahead: Fix Them Now or Pay for It Later*. Washington, DC: AASHTO, 2009. http://roughroads.transportation.org/RoughRoads_FullReport.pdf.

Aultman-Hall, Lisa, Jonathan Dowds, and Brian Y. Lee. "Innovative Data Collection for Pedestrians, Bicycles, and Other Non–Motor Vehicle Modes," *TR News* 280 (May–June 2012).

Badger, Emily. "Everything You Ever Wanted to Know about Bus Rapid Transit." *Atlantic Cities*, April 2, 2012. http://www.theatlanticcities.com/commute/2012/04/how-build-better-brt-system/1647.

Baldwin, Peter. *Fighting Traffic: The Dawn of the Motor Age in the American City*. Cambridge, MA: MIT Press, 2011.

Birk, Mia. *Joyride: Pedaling toward a Healthier Planet*. Portland, OR: Cadence, 2010.

Bleier, Asha, Kathleen Ferrier, Andy Hamilton, Greg Konar, Brooke Peterson, Dave Sorenson, and Seth Torma. *From Policy to Pavement: Implementing Complete Streets in the San Diego Region*. San Diego: American Planning Association of California/Walk San Diego, 2012. http://www.calapa.org/attachments/files/1851/APA_Report_Final_compressed.pdf.

Boston Transportation Department. "Boston Complete Streets Guidelines." Draft (undated). http://bostoncompletestreets.org.

Caltrans. *Caltrans Highway Design Manual Update (Complete Streets Update)* (May 2012).

Campbell, Bob, Charles V. Zegeer, Herman H. Huang, and Michael J. Cynecki. *A Review of Pedestrian Safety Research in the United States and Abroad*. Federal Highway Administration, 2004.

Carmalt, Charles. *Constructing, Maintaining and Financing Sidewalks in New Jersey*. New Brunswick, NJ: Alan M. Voorhees Transportation Center, 2006.

Centers for Disease Control and Prevention. *Recommended Community Strategies and Measurements to Prevent Obesity in the United States* (2009). http://www.ncbi.nlm.nih.gov/pubmed/19629029.

Charlotte Department of Transportation. *Urban Street Design Guidelines* (2007). http://
charmeck.org/city/charlotte/transportation/plansprojects/pages/urban%20
street%20design%20guidelines.aspx.

City of Chicago. *Complete Streets Chicago: Design Guidelines* (2013). http://www.cityof
chicago.org/city/en/depts/cdot/provdrs/future_projects_andconcepts/news/2013
/mar/complete_streetsdesignguidelines.html.

City of Dallas. *Complete Streets Design Manual*. Draft, July 2012. http://www.scribd.com
/doc/102019169/Dallas-Complete-Streets-Design-Manual-Draft-July-2012.

City of Nashville. *Major and Collector Street Plan* (2012). http://maps.nashville.gov/mcsp.

City of Philadelphia Streets Department. *Philadelphia Complete Streets Design Handbook*
(2013). http://philadelphiastreets.com/handbook.aspx.

Clifton, Kelly, Sarah Bronstein, and Sara Morrissey. "The Adoption of Complete Streets in
Transportation-Disadvantaged Communities: Lessons from US Case Studies." Paper
13-4615. *Proceedings, Transportation Research Board Annual Meeting, 2013.* http://
amonline.trb.org.

———. *The Path to Complete Streets in Underserved Communities: Lessons from US Case Studies.*
Portland, OR: Portland State University, 2013. http://www.smartgrowthamerica.org
/documents/cs/resources/complete-streets-in-underserved-communities.pdf.

Cortright, Joe. *Driven Apart: How Sprawl Is Lengthening Our Commutes and Why Misleading
Mobility Measures Are Making Things Worse.* CEOs for Cities, September 2010. http://
www.ceosforcities.org/research/driven-apart.

———. *Portland's Green Dividend.* CEOs for Cities, July 2007. http://www.ceosforcities.org
/city-dividends/green/special-reports/portland.

Dannenberg, Andrew, Howard Frumkin, and Richard J. Jackson, eds. *Making Healthy
Places: Designing and Building for Health, Well-Being, and Sustainability.* Washington, DC:
Island Press, 2011.

Dill, Jennifer, and Theresa Carr. "Bicycle Commuting and Facilities in Major US Cities: If
You Build Them, Commuters Will Use Them." *Transportation Research Record: Journal
of the Transportation Research Board* 1828 (2003): 116–23.

Dumbaugh, Eric. "Safe Streets, Livable Streets." *Journal of the American Planning Association*
71 (2005): 283–300.

Ewing, Reid, and Robert Cervero. "Travel and the Built Environment: A Meta-Analysis."
Journal of the American Planning Association 76, no. 3 (2010): 265–94.

Ewing, Reid, and Eric Dumbaugh. "The Built Environment and Traffic Safety: A Review
of Empirical Evidence." *Journal of Planning Literature* 23, no. 4 (2009).

Ewing, Reid, Tom Schmid, Richard Killingsworth, Amy Zlot, and Stephen Raudenbush.
"Relationship between Urban Sprawl and Physical Activity, Obesity, and Morbidity."
American Journal of Health Promotion 18, no. 1 (2003): 47–57.

Federal Highway Administration. "Evaluation of Lane Reduction 'Road Diet' Measures on
Crashes: Summary Report." Pub. no. FHWA-HRT-10-053. Highway Safety Information System, 2010. http://www.fhwa.dot.gov/publications/research
/safety/10053/10053.pdf.

———. *Pedestrian Safety Guide for Transit Agencies* (2008). FHWA-SA-07-017. http://safety
.fhwa.dot.gov/ped_bike/ped_transit/ped_transguide/ch1.cfm.

———. *Summary of Travel Trends: 2009 National Household Travel Survey* (June 2011). http://
nhts.ornl.gov/2009/pub/stt.pdf.

Ferrier, Kathleen, Andy Hamilton, and Greg Konar. *Safe for All: 2011 Street Design Benchmark Study for the San Diego Region.* Walk San Diego, 2011. http://www.walksandiego
.org/resources/publications.

Frank, Lawrence, Michael Greenwald, Sarah Kasage, and Andrew Devlin. *An Assessment of Urban Form and Pedestrian and Transit Improvements as an Integrated GHG Reduction Strategy.* Washington State DOT Research Report, WA-RD 765.1. Olympia: Washington State DOT, April 2011. http://www.wsdot.wa.gov/research/reports/fullreports/765.1.pdf.

Frumkin, Howard, Lawrence Frank, and Richard Jackson. *Urban Sprawl and Public Health: Designing, Planning, and Building for Healthy Communities.* Washington, DC: Island Press, 2004.

Furie, Greg, and M. M. Desai. "Active Transportation and Cardiovascular Disease Risk Factors in U.S. Adults." *American Journal of Preventive Medicine* 43 (2012): 621–28.

Geller, Roger. *How Portland Benefits from Bicycle Transportation.* Portland Bureau of Transportation (undated). http://www.portlandoregon.gov/transportation/article/371038.

Gladwell, Malcolm. *The Tipping Point.* New York: Little, Brown, 2000.

Grant, Michael, Harrison Rue, Stephanie Trainor, Jocelyn Bauer, Jamie Parks, Mary Raulerson, Kathleen Rooney, and Sonya Suter. *The Role of Transportation Systems Management and Operations in Supporting Livability and Sustainability: A Primer.* Washington, DC: Federal Highway Administration, 2012. http://www.ops.fhwa.dot.gov/publications/fhwahop12004/fhwahop12004.pdf.

Handy, Susan, and Barbara McCann. "The Regional Response to Federal Funding for Bicycle and Pedestrian Projects." *Journal of the American Planning Association* 77, no. 1 (2010): 23–38.

Handy, Susan L., Barbara McCann, Linda Bailey, Michelle Ernst, Lanier McRee, Emily Meharg, Reid Ewing, and Kate Wright. *The Regional Response to Federal Funding for Bicycle and Pedestrian Projects.* Davis: Institute of Transportation Studies, University of California, Davis, 2009.

Harnik, Peter. *Urban Green: Innovative Parks for Resurgent Cities.* Washington, DC: Island Press, 2012.

Huang, Terry T, Adam Drewnowski, Shiriki K. Kumanyika, and Thomas A. Glass. "A Systems-Oriented Multilevel Framework for Addressing Obesity in the 21st Century." *Preventing Chronic Disease* 6, no. 3 (2009). http://www.cdc.gov/pcd/issues/2009/jul/09_0013.htm.

Institute for Transportation Engineers. *Designing Walkable Urban Thoroughfares: A Context-Sensitive Approach.* Washington, DC: Institute of Transportation Engineers, 2010. http://www.ite.org/emodules/scriptcontent/Orders/ProductDetail.cfm?pc=RP-036A-E.

Jackson, Kenneth T. *Crabgrass Frontier: The Suburbanization of the United States.* New York: Oxford University Press, 1987.

Jacobsen, Peter. "Safety in Numbers: More Walkers and Bicyclists, Safer Walking and Bicycling." *Injury Prevention* 9 (2003): 205–9.

Jaffe, Eric. "The Transportation Planning Rule Every City Should Reform." *Atlantic Cities,* December 5, 2011. http://www.theatlanticcities.com/commute/2011/12/transportation-planning-law-every-city-should-repeal/636.

Jones, Michael G., Sherry Ryan, Jennifer Donlon, Lauren Ledbetter, David R. Ragland, and Lindsay Arnold. *Measuring Bicycle and Pedestrian Activity in San Diego County and Its Relationship to Land Use, Transportation, Safety, and Facility Type.* Berkeley: University of California, Berkeley, Safe Transportation Research and Education Center, 2010.

Kastenhofer, Ilona. O. *An Examination of Practices for Retrofitting Existing Roads with Sidewalks in the United States.* VTRC 10-R4. Charlottesville: Virginia Transportation Research Council, 2010.

Kim, Annette M. "Unimaginable Change." *Journal of the American Planning Association* 77, no. 4 (2011): 328–37.

Leaf, W. A., and D. F. Preusser. "Literature Review on Vehicle Travel Speeds and Pedestrian Injuries among Selected Racial/Ethnic Groups." U.S. Department of Transportation, National Highway Traffic Safety Administration (1999).

Leinberger, Christopher. *The Option of Urbanism: Investing in a New American Dream.* Washington, DC: Island Press, 2009.

Leinberger, Christopher, and Mariela Alfonzo. *Walk This Way: The Economic Promise of Walkable Places in Metropolitan Washington, D.C.* Brookings Institution, May 2012. http://www.brookings.edu/research/papers/2012/05/25-walkable-places-leinberger.

Lenker, James A., and Jordana L. Maisel. "The Best and Worst of Complete Streets: Lessons Learned from 13 Municipalities." P13-6290. Presentation at the annual meeting of the Transportation Research Board, January 13, 2013. http://amonline.trb.org.

Lewis, Tom. *Divided Highways.* New York: Penguin, 1997.

Litman, Todd. *Evaluating Complete Streets: The Value of Designing Roads for Diverse Modes, Users and Activities.* Victoria Transport Policy Institute, March 15, 2013. http://www.vtpi.org/compstr.pdf.

———. *Evaluating Non-motorized Transportation Benefits and Costs.* Victoria Transport Policy Institute, March 24, 2013. http://www.vtpi.org/nmt-tdm.pdf.

———. *Short and Sweet: Analysis of Shorter Trips Using National Personal Travel Survey Data.* Victoria, BC: Victoria Transport Policy Institute, 2012. www.vtpi.org/NHTS_2009.xls.

Los Angeles County. *Model Design Manual for Living Streets* (2011). http://www.modelstreetdesignmanual.com/index.html.

Louisville Metro Government. *Complete Streets Manual* (October 2007). http://www.louisvilleky.gov/BikeLouisville/Complete+Streets.

Lynott, Jana, Amanda Taylor, Hannah Twaddell, Jessica Haase, Kristin Nelson, Jared Ulmer, Barbara McCann, and Edward R. Stollof. *Planning Complete Streets for an Aging America.* Washington, DC: AARP, 2009.

MacDonald, Elizabeth, Rebecca Sanders, and Alia Anderson. "Performance Measures for Complete, Green Streets: A Proposal for Urban Arterials in California." Final report. University of California Transportation Center, July 28, 2009. http://www.dot.ca.gov/hq/LandArch/research/docs/Complete_Streets_Performance_Measures.pdf.

Maizlish, Neil, James Woodcock, Sean Co, Bart Ostro, Amir Fanai, and David Fairley. "Health Cobenefits and Transportation-Related Reductions in Greenhouse Gas Emissions in the San Francisco Bay Area." *American Journal of Public Health* 103 (2013): 703–9.

Marshall, Wesley, and Norman Garrick. "Street Network Types and Road Safety: A Study of 24 California Cities." *Urban Design International* 15 (2010): 133–47.

Massachusetts Department of Transportation. *Project Development and Design Guide* (January 2006). http://www.mhd.state.ma.us/default.asp?pgid=content/designguide&sid=about.

McCann, Barbara. *Complete Streets Report: Analysis of a Survey of Complete Streets Laws, Policies, and Plans in the United States.* Washington, DC: Thunderhead Alliance, 2004. (Thunderhead is now the Alliance for Biking and Walking.)

McCann, Barbara, and Reid Ewing. *Measuring the Health Effects of Sprawl: A National Analysis of Physical Activity, Obesity and Chronic Disease.* Washington, DC: Smart Growth America, 2003. http://www.smartgrowthamerica.org/research/measuring-the-health-effects-of-sprawl.

McCann, Barbara, Lanier McRee, Susan L. Handy, Emily Meharg, Linda Bailey, Reid

Ewing, Michelle Ernst, and Kate Wright. *The Regional Response to Federal Funding for Bicycle and Pedestrian Projects: Executive Summary.* Research Report UCD-ITS-RR-09-22. Institute of Transportation Studies, University of California, Davis, 2009. http://pubs.its.ucdavis.edu/publication_detail.php?id=1311.

McCann, Barbara, and Suzanne Rynne. *Complete Streets: Best Policy and Implementation Practices.* Planners Advisory Service Report #559. Chicago: American Planning Association, 2010.

McCann, Barbara, and Stefanie Seskin. *Complete Streets: Guide to Tackling the Cost Question.* National Complete Streets Coalition/Centers for Disease Control and Prevention, forthcoming 2013. http://www.smartgrowthamerica.org/complete-streets/complete-streets-fundamentals/factsheets/costs.

Mid-America Regional Council. *Complete Streets Handbook* (2012). http://marc.org/transportation/pdf/CompleteStreetsHandbook.pdf.

National Association of City Transportation Officials. *Urban Bikeway Design Guide.* Washington, DC: Island Press, 2012, http://nacto.org/cities-for-cycling/design-guide.

———. *Urban Street Design Guide,* October 2012. http://www.nyc.gov/html/dot/downloads/pdf/2012-nacto-urban-street-design-guide.pdf.

National Complete Streets Coalition. *Getting Results: Complete Streets in Minnesota* (2012). http://www.smartgrowthamerica.org/documents/cs/resources/cs-in-minnesota.pdf.

National Complete Streets Coalition and Local Government Commission. *It's a Safe Decision: Complete Streets in California* (2012). http://www.smartgrowthamerica.org/2012/02/28/complete-streets-success-stories-focus-of-new-report.

Nelson, Arthur C. *Reshaping Metropolitan America: Development Trends and Opportunities to 2030.* Washington, DC: Island Press, 2013.

New Jersey Bicycle and Pedestrian Resource Center. *Constructing, Maintaining, and Financing Sidewalks in New Jersey* (2008). http://www.njbikeped.org/index.php?module=Downloads&func=prep_hand_out&lid=1513.

New York City Department of Transportation. *Measuring the Street: New Metrics for 21st Century Streets* (November 2012). http://www.nyc.gov/html/dot/downloads/pdf/2012-10-measuring-the-street.pdf.

———. *Sustainable Streets Plan* (2008). http://www.nyc.gov/html/dot/html/about/strat plan.shtml.

Nicholls, Jim. *State Highways as Main Streets: A Study of Community Design and Visioning.* WA-RD 733.1. Washington State Department of Transportation/University of Washington Research for FHWA, 2009. http://www.wsdot.wa.gov/research/reports/fullreports/733.1.pdf.

North Carolina Department of Transportation (NCDOT). *NCDOT Complete Streets Planning and Design Guidelines.* NCDOT, 2012. http://www.completestreetsnc.org.

Potts, Ingrid B., Douglas Harwood, and Karen Richard. "Relationship of Lane Width to Safety for Urban and Suburban Arterials." Paper presented at the annual meeting of the Transportation Research Board, Washington, DC, January 2007.

Pratt, Richard H., Jay Evans, Herbert Levinson, Shawn Turner, C. Y. Jeng, and Daniel Nabors. "Pedestrian and Bicycle Facilities." Chap. 16 in *Traveler Response to Transportation System Changes Handbook.* TCRP Report 95. Washington, DC: Transportation Research Board, 2012.

Pucher, John, and Ralph Buehler, eds. *City Cycling.* Cambridge, MA: MIT Press, 2012.

Repair Priorities: Transportation Spending Strategies to Save Taxpayer Dollars and Improve Roads. Washington, DC: Smart Growth America/Taxpayers for Common Sense, June 2011. http://www.smartgrowthamerica.org/repair-priorities.

Rodriguez, Daniel. *Active Transportation: Making the Link from Transportation to Physical Activity and Obesity: A Research Brief.* Princeton, NJ: Active Living Research, 2009. http://activelivingresearch.org/node/12296.

Rogers, Everett M. *Diffusion of Innovations.* New York: Free Press, 1995.

Sam Schwartz Engineering and America Walks. *Steps to a Walkable Community: A Guide for Citizens, Planners, and Engineers* (2012). http://americawalks.org/2012/09/america-walks-and-sam-schwartz-engineering-release-steps-to-a-walkable-community.

San Francisco Planning Department. "San Francisco Better Streets Plan" (2010). http://www.sf-planning.org/ftp/BetterStreets/proposals.htm#Final_Plan.

Seskin, Stefanie. *Complete Streets Local Policy Workbook.* Smart Growth America/National Complete Streets Coalition, August 2012. http://www.smartgrowthamerica.org/documents/cs-local-policy-workbook.pdf.

———. *Complete Streets Policy Analysis 2011: Inclusive. Diverse. Accountable.* Washington, DC: Smart Growth America/National Complete Streets Coalition, 2012. http://www.smartgrowthamerica.org/documents/cs/cs-2011-policyanalysis.pdf.

Seskin, Stefanie, and Lily Gordon-Koven. *The Best Complete Streets Policies of 2012.* Washington, DC: Smart Growth America/National Complete Streets Coalition, 2013. http://www.smartgrowthamerica.org/documents/cs-2012-policy-analysis.pdf.

Shapard, James, and Mark Cole. "Do Complete Streets Cost More than Incomplete Streets?" Paper 13-4283. *Proceedings, Transportation Research Board Annual Meeting, 2013.* http://amonline.trb.org/2ve3qr/1.

Shinkle, Douglas. *On the Move: State Strategies for 21st Century Transportation Solutions.* National Conference of State Legislatures, 2012. http://www.ncsl.org/documents/transportation/On-THE-MOVE.pdf.

Shoup, Lilly, Nick Donohue, and Marisa Lang. *The Fix We're In For: The State of Our Bridges.* Transportation for America, 2011. http://t4america.org/resources/bridges/overview.

Smart Growth America and State Smart Transportation Initiative. *The Innovative DOT: A Handbook of Policy and Practice.* Washington, DC: Smart Growth America, 2012. http://www.smartgrowthamerica.org/the-innovative-dot.

Smith, Ken R., Barbara B. Brown, Ikuho Yamada, Lori Kowaleski-Jones, Cathleen D. Zick, and Jessie X. Fan. "Walkability and Body Mass Index: Density, Design, and New Diversity Measures." *American Journal of Preventive Medicine* 35 (2008): 237–44.

Smith, Kevin B., and Christopher W. Larimer. *The Public Policy Theory Primer.* Boulder, CO: Westview, 2009.

Southworth, Michael, and Eran Ben-Joseph. *Streets and the Shaping of Towns and Cities.* Washington, DC: Island Press, 2003.

Tomer, Adie. *Transit Access and Zero-Vehicle Households.* Washington, DC: Brookings Institution, 2012. http://www.brookings.edu/~/media/Files/rc/papers/2011/0818_transportation_tomer/0818_transportation_tomer.pdf.

Toth, Gary. *A Citizen's Guide to Better Streets: How to Engage your Transportation Agency.* New York: Project for Public Spaces, 2008. http://www.pps.org/pdf/bookstore/How_to_Engage_Your_Transportation_Agency_AARP.pdf.

Transportation for America. *Dangerous by Design: Solving the Epidemic of Preventable Pedestrian Deaths.* Smart Growth America, 2011. http://t4america.org/resources/dangerousbydesign2011.

Tumlin, Jeffrey. *Sustainable Transportation Planning: Tools for Creating Vibrant, Healthy, and Resilient Communities.* Hoboken, NJ: Wiley, 2012.

United States Access Board. *Revised Draft Guidelines for Accessible Public Rights-of-Way* (November 2005). http://www.access-board.gov/prowac/draft.htm.

Urgo, John, Meredith Wilensky, and Steven Weissman. *Moving beyond Prevailing Street De-sign Standards: Assessing Legal and Liability Barrier to More Efficient Street Design and Func-tion.* Berkeley: University of California, Berkeley, December 2010. http://www.crec
.berkeley.edu/crec.whitepaper.pdf.

U.S. Department of Justice. *ADA Best Practices Tool Kit for State and Local Governments* (2007). http://www.ada.gov/pcatoolkit/toolkitmain.htm.

U.S. Government Accountability Office. *Bus Rapid Transit: Projects Improve Transit Service and Can Contribute to Economic Development* (July 2012). GAO-12-811. http://www.gao
.gov/products/GAO-12-811.

U.S. PIRG Education Fund. *Do Roads Pay for Themselves? Setting the Record Straight on Transportation Funding* (January 2011). http://www.uspirg.org/reports/usf/do-roads
-pay-themselves.

Walkable and Livable Communities Institute and AARP. "From Inspiration to Action: Implementing Projects to Support Active Living" (undated). http://www.walklive
.org/project/implementation-guide.

Walker, Jarrett. *Human Transit: How Clearer Thinking about Public Transit Can Enrich Our Communities and Our Lives.* Washington, DC: Island Press, 2012.

Walsh, Ryan. *Local Policies and Practices That Support Safe Pedestrian Environments: A Synthe-sis of Highway Practice.* National Cooperative Highway Research Program Synthesis 436. Washington, DC: Transportation Research Board, 2012. http://apps.trb.org
/cmsfeed/TRBNetProjectDisplay.asp?ProjectID=2947.

Weinstein Agrawal, Asha, Hilary Nixon, and Vinay Murthy. *What Do Americans Think about Federal Tax Options to Support Public Transit, Highways, and Local Streets and Roads? Results from Year 3 of a National Survey.* MTI Report 12-01. San Jose, CA: Mineta Trans-portation Institute, 2012. http://transweb.sjsu.edu/PDFs/research/1128-american
-survey-federal-taxes-public-transit-highways-streets-roads.pdf.

Wieters, Kathleen Meghan, Jan Fees, and Barbara McCann. "Why Should We Care about Those Silly Pedestrians and Bicyclists? Barriers to Adoption of Complete Streets Or-dinances in Cowboy Country." Abstract #712. Paper presented at the Association of Collegiate Schools of Planning, Cincinnati, OH, November 1–4, 2012.

Wykle, Kenneth. *Accommodating Bicycle and Pedestrian Travel: A Recommended Approach.* Washington, DC: Federal Highway Administration, 2000. http://www.fhwa.dot.gov
/environment/bicycle_pedestrian/guidance/design_guidance/design.cfm.

Index

through infrastructure repair projects,
134
lasting value weighed in, 141–142,
143f, 144–146
planning ahead for, 134–135
road, 131–132, 145
safety, 129, 131–132
traffic congestion economic, 122
variability, 135–137
crosswalk, 1, 46f, 128, 151, 156
culture
policy and values for change in, 4, 19,
28–29, 93, 108, 121transportation
and divide in, 16–18
transportation change through, 4,
18–19, 76, 122–123

Dannemiller, Mike, 109
data collection
"before and after" impact, 80–81
community and counting, 79–81
complete streets research lacking, 79
multimodal transportation, 80
politics and, 79
success measurement and, 78–81
Davis, Sheree, 76, 121, 141
Dean, Karl, 119–120, 121
death, 1, 15, 33, 43, 48, 49, 129, 141
decision-making. *See also* transportation
agencies
changing systems of, 54
complete street champion
understanding of, 107–108
complete street champions facilitating,
106
design manual and tools for, 72, 74–75
education and training on, 76
inclusive, 108, 139–140
politicians' transportation, 24
public and public advocacy in, 58–59,
110–111
transportation and considerations in,
68–70, 69f
understanding the process of, 60–62
Denney, Charlie, 100
design. *See* road and road system
design manual

changing, 71–75
at community and city level, 73–74
complete streets, 31–32, 140
"cookbook" use approach to, 17
decision-making tools in, 72, 74–75
education provided by, 73–74
Green Book, 15, 17, 19, 72
resources for, 72, 174
state-level, 72–74
time spent in rewriting, 71–72
on transportation-land use connection,
74
uniform road construction, 14–15
development, 54–71. *See also* private
development
departments of transportation. *See*
state department of transportation;
transportation agencies
diffusion innovation theory, 27–28
disabled, 48–49, 49f, 109, 152–153
diversity of advocacy coalition, 26–27,
38–39
DOT. *See* state department of
transportation, transportation
agencies
drivers, user priority, 150–151
Duluth, MN, 57–58, 115
Dumbaugh, Eric, 44
Dyrdahl, Matt, 90–91

economy, 35, 122, 144–145
education and training
broad, 54
decision-making, 76
design manual providing, 73–74
in implementation, 75–77
from National Complete Streets
Coalition, 76–77
for public and public advocacy, 77, 114,
115, 124–126
for transportation agencies and
professionals, 75–77
engineers
planners/urban designers' cultural
divide with, 16–18
as problem solvers, 123–124
as project-driven, 16–17

priority. *See* user priority
private development, 90–92, 157
problem-solving, engineer, 123–124
projects, complete streets
 in Charlotte, 124–126, 125f
 complete street holistic mix of, 85
 complete streets policy *versus*, 24,
  53–54, 85, 160
 cost reduction in, 134
 development, starting over, 69–71
 development changes for, 54–71
 limits set for, 135
 maintenance and operations, 65–66,
  107
 MPOs funding and selection of, 88,
  161–162
 opposition to, 91, 109–110, 111–112,
  157
 pedestrian, 142, 143f, 144
 public support built through
  noncontroversial, 113–114
 spending prioritization systems for,
  161–163
 teams for, 57
 transportation industry and engineers
  driven by, 16–17, 24
PSE. *See* Policy-Systems-Environmental
 change model
public and public advocacy
 complete streets champion
  engagement of, 110–115
 complete streets decisions and, 58–59,
  110–111
 complete streets funding through,
  137–139
 complete streets research on, 112–113
 documentation of support from, 112
 education and training for, 77, 114,
  115, 124–126
 incremental change for, 98
 leadership relationship with, 115–116
 maintenance and lesser involvement
  of, 94
 projects lacking controversy first in
  building, 113–114
 transportation agency/professional
  relationship with, 110–111

public health, advocates, and community
 complete streets support from and
  benefit to, 33, 35, 60, 61–62, 110,
  119–120, 142, 163–164, 169
 as transportation change model,
  13–14, 19
public transportation
 bus stops, 33–34, 84f, 57, 58f
 in Cleveland, 158–159
 interest rising for, 3
 funding, 10–11, 140, 155
 low-income riders of, 156
 in multimodal network, 13
 paratransit, 97, 140
 silos, breaking down, 59
 space for, 14, 73, 155–156
 user priority, 155–156
public works, 93–94, 95–96, 121

Ratekin, Chris, 108
Reid, Don, 95–96
relationship building, 103–104, 105–106,
 107, 110, 121–124
research, 16, 44, 46, 47, 49. *See also*
 complete streets research
resources
 complete streets financial, 137–140
 complete streets fundamental, 174
 design manual, 72
 help and involvement, 175
 for implementation, 175
 writing and adoption, 174–175
revenue. *See* funding and revenue
road and road system. *See also* funding
 and revenue
 complete streets research on
  disadvantaged users of, 163–164
 conditions, 93
 cost, 131–132
 maintenance and conversion of, 96–97,
  96f, 98–99, 124–126
 multimodal network approach to,
  13–14, 23, 71, 85, 138, 150–151,
  160–161, 163, 169
 operation of, 96–97, 96f
 public transportation and lanes in,
  155–156